Home Office Research Study 254

The nature of personal robbery

Jonathan Smith

Home Office Research, Development and Statistics Directorate
January 2003

Home Office Research Studies

The Home Office Research Studies are reports on research undertaken by or on behalf of the Home Office. They cover the range of subjects for which the Home Secretary has responsibility. Other publications produced by the Research, Development and Statistics Directorate include Findings, Statistical Bulletins and Statistical Papers.

The Research, Development and Statistics Directorate

RDS is part of the Home Office. The Home Office's purpose is to build a safe, just and tolerant society in which the rights and responsibilities of individuals, families and communities are properly balanced and the protection and security of the public are maintained.

RDS is also part of National Statistics (NS). One of the aims of NS is to inform Parliament and the citizen about the state of the nation and provide a window on the work and performance of government, allowing the impact of government policies and actions to be assessed.

Therefore –

Research Development and Statistics Directorate exists to improve policy making, decision taking and practice in support of the Home Office purpose and aims, to provide the public and Parliament with information necessary for informed debate and to publish information for future use.

First published 2003
Application for reproduction should be made to the Communication Development Unit, Room 201, Home Office, 50 Queen Anne's Gate, London SW1H 9AT.
© Crown copyright 2003   ISBN 1 84082 909 5
                          ISSN 0072 6435

Foreword

The growth in recorded robbery offences over recent years has justifiably been a cause of considerable concern. Developing an evidence-base that goes well beyond those disturbing high profile cases that receive national attention is an essential part of the process of developing an effective response to this problem. Through a detailed examination of police case files, this study paints a detailed and vivid picture of the nature of personal robbery, the characteristics of victims, offenders and the robbery event itself. What emerges is a complex and changing problem that varies in time and place. In conjunction with other research on the detailed operational responses to personal robbery, this work will do much to help our improving understanding of, and responses to, personal robbery.

DAVID MOXON
Research, Development and Statistics

Acknowledgements

This research could not have been undertaken without the generous co-operation of a number of police forces who kindly provided the time and space for a team of RDS researchers to sift through and collect information from the robbery case files. RDS is particularly grateful to the Metropolitan Police who speedily dealt with numerous requests for information, and to staff at Stockport Police Station in Greater Manchester whose advice and expertise proved invaluable in the design and setting up of the research.

Several researchers across RDS provided assistance with the data collection for this report. Particular thanks go to Joe Mayhew and Rebecca Sheehan in finalising and quality assuring the final data set, to Geoff Newiss, Jon Simmons, Pat Mayhew and Victoria Harrington for their assistance throughout the course of the research, and to Andy Feist whose input and considered advice have proved invaluable.

RDS would like to thank Professor Martin Gill from Leicester University who acted as independent assessor to the report.

Jonathan Smith

Contents

List of figures

List of tables

Summary

Against a background of overall reductions in recorded crime in recent years in England and Wales, annual increases in robberies stand out as a disturbing counter trend. Although robberies against the person, and street crime generally, constitute a very small proportion of overall crime, there is plenty of evidence to suggest that anxiety over these crimes contributes to general anxieties over crime and policing in Britain today. Behind the headline statistics, our knowledge of the nature of robbery, and personal robbery in particular, has been limited. This study has aimed to address this gap, through a detailed examination of several thousand police case files.

This report examines the nature of robbery in England and Wales, based on an examination of over 2,000 crime reports and witness statements across seven police force areas. The report focuses specifically on personal robbery, which accounts for the bulk of recorded robbery and almost all of the increase in recent years.

Overview of robbery in England and Wales

- There have been marked increases in the level of recorded robbery in recent years. Between April 2001 and March 2002, robbery increased by 28 per cent, or 26,221 offences. This followed a 13 per cent rise the previous year, and a 26 per cent increase the year before that (an increase of 10,877 and 17,441 offences respectively). Personal robbery accounts for the bulk of recorded robbery in England and Wales.

- Robbery is concentrated in relatively few police force areas, and predominately in urban metropolitan forces. The ten police forces currently part of the Street Crime Initiative accounted for 83 per cent of all recorded robbery between April 2001 and March 2002. The Metropolitan Police Service dominates this picture, accounting for 44 per cent of all recorded robbery in England and Wales.

- Robbery, however, is disproportionately concentrated in a smaller number of basic command units (BCUs) when compared to other crime types such as burglary and violent crime in general. Just 7 per cent of BCUs in England and Wales accounted for 42 per cent of recorded robberies between April 2001 and March 2002. This is far in excess of any other crime type.

- A limited comparison with other jurisdictions suggests that England and Wales now have one of the highest levels of recorded robberies per population, overtaking the United States which has seen a 28 per cent reduction in robbery since 1996 and a 47 per cent reduction since 1990. There were 86 recorded robberies per 100,000 population in Scotland in 2000 compared to 160 in England and Wales.

Characteristics of suspects and victims

- A high proportion of personal robbery involves young persons as victims and offenders. Two out of every five personal robberies involved a victim and an offender under the age of 21 years. Victims over the age of 61 years accounted for just 5 per cent of victims. Just over half of all offenders were aged between 16 and 20 years.

- There has been a marked increase in younger victims and offenders over the last ten years. Information obtained from the Metropolitan Police shows that in 2000, 11-15 year-olds accounted for 25 per cent of all victims, and 16-20 year-olds accounted for 22 per cent. By contrast, in 1993 these two age groups accounted for 12 per cent and 13 per cent respectively of all personal robbery victims. The proportion of suspects aged 11-15 years increased from 15 per cent in 1993 to 36 per cent in 2000.

- The younger age profile for robbery offences is not matched for other offence types. Information from the Metropolitan Police shows that those charged with offences of personal robbery where typically younger than those charged with other offences, such as burglary and violence against the person.

- Offenders and victims are predominantly male. 76 per cent of victims were male, although there were some variations between different BCUs. Suspects are overwhelmingly male (94%) and there was little variation between the BCUs sampled. Female offending in personal robbery is relatively rare, accounting for only 6 per cent of suspects. Seven out of ten robberies involved male victims being attacked by male suspects. One in five robberies (21%) involved female victims attacked by male suspects.

- Robberies were most commonly committed by two or more persons acting together. Younger male victims were more likely to be targeted by groups of offenders, and females by an offender acting alone.

- The BCU data showed marked contrasts in the ethnic make-up of robbery suspects reflecting, in part, local population differences. In six of the nine BCUs sampled, victims described their attackers as 'black' in the majority of cases. Comparisons with local population estimates suggest that visible ethnic minorities are over represented, but this is also true of minority ethnic victims in some of the BCUs sampled. These findings cannot be extrapolated to provide any national picture, neither is the true number of offenders certain. Research published elsewhere does, however, draw similar conclusions.

- Most personal robberies were reported to the police within the hour, but a sizeable proportion take longer; 18 per cent took between one and four hours and 16 per cent took more than 8 hours to report. Of those contacting the police, 45 per cent of personal robberies were reported via a '999' call and a further 7 per cent were reported to passing patrols. 16 per cent were reported to the police via a non-emergency telephone, and 28 per cent were reported at the front desk of the local police station. Delayed reporting may be due to fear and shock at what has happened, for instance. But it is also true that victim characteristics appear to be related to reporting behaviours; retired victims were more likely to report immediately via a '999' call, while students and unemployed persons were more likely to report at the front desk. Robberies involving mobile phones were more likely to involve delayed reporting, which may be related in part to the need to obtain a crime number for insurance purposes.

The robbery event

- Typically, personal robbery is more likely to occur at night. Half (51%) of all robberies occurred between the hours of 6 p.m. and 2 a.m., and half again (49%) occurred at the weekend.

- School-aged and retired victims were most likely to be offended against during the daytime (67% and 61% respectively), in marked contrast to the overall picture of victims typically being targeted at night. Over half (54%) of school-aged victims were robbed during the afternoon period between 2 p.m. and 6 p.m.

- A large number of personal robberies occurred in open public spaces, primarily a street, but also footpaths, alleyways, subways and parks. That said, almost 40 per cent of personal robberies occurred either in or around locations other than a street, such as commercial premises or while the victim was using some form of transport.

- In the two British Transport Police (BTP) areas covering the London Underground and the South East, over half (56%) of all personal robberies occurred in the carriage of a train or tube train.

- Victims were typically targeted in one of four different ways by their attackers. These are referred to in the analysis as 'blitz', 'confrontation', 'con' and 'snatch' robberies.

- A confrontation was the most frequent method by which victims were targeted by suspects, accounting for over a third of all robberies (37%). The blitz approach accounted for a quarter (25%), and a slightly lower proportion (22%) of robberies were preceded by the 'con'. Snatch robberies accounted for 14 per cent, while victim initiated robberies made up just a small proportion (2%).

- Confrontation and con robberies were more common among younger and male victims, and snatch robberies much more common among female victims. Over one in five personal robberies in this sample involved victims aged between 11 and 20 years in a confrontation. This is by far the most prevalent of all types of robbery.

- Weapons were used or displayed in just over a third of personal robberies (33%) and more so where the offender's approach to the victim was one of confrontation (45%). Snatch robberies rarely involved the use of a weapon, as would be expected. Knives were the most common weapon type, and were used in 21 per cent of personal robberies; guns were used in just 3 per cent of cases.

- Two out of every five personal robberies resulted in injury of some sort to the victim. This was particularly the case in blitz and snatch robberies, and least likely in confrontation robberies. These differences can be explained by the more frequent use of weapons in confrontation robberies, by the fact that blitz robberies are by their nature always violent, by the greater involvement of female victims in snatch robberies, and by female victims' greater tendency to struggle with their attacker.

- Robbery was more physically intrusive for male victims than for female victims. Male victims were more likely than female victims to be physically searched by their attackers, and forced to hand over their property or turn out their pockets. Over seven out of ten robberies of female victims involved the property being snatched or grabbed from around their person.

- While cash is most likely to be stolen from the victim during personal robbery, over two in every five personal robberies involved a mobile phone being stolen or demanded from the victim (43%). There were differences between BCUs. The two BTP areas covering the London Underground and the South East had the largest proportion of personal robberies involving mobile phones. Younger victims under the age of 21 years were more likely to have a mobile phone stolen than older age groups.

- Over a quarter of mobile phone robberies, representing 12 per cent of all personal robbery in this sample, occurred while the victim was using their phone or had it on display. There is some evidence that these groups and younger victims were specifically targeted for their mobile phones. The analysis of victim statements suggest that involvement in mobile phone robbery is as much to do with the desirability of the handset as a fashion item, as any other possible motivation.

Section 5 addresses the implications of these findings for the way in which police and other agencies tailor their responses to the robbery problem.

1.   Introduction

Recorded offences of robbery have risen sharply in recent years despite the fact that recorded crime overall has fallen over the same period. Between April 2001 and March 2002 robbery offences recorded by the police increased by 28 per cent. This followed a 13 per cent increase the previous year, and a 26 per cent increase before that (Simmons *et al*, 2002). High profile publicity of what one national newspaper earlier in 2002 described as a "rash of horrific street crimes" (Sunday Telegraph, January 2002) focused attention on the upward rise in recorded robbery and street crime more generally. Although headlines featuring more extreme cases may not accurately describe the overall nature of robbery, coverage of them demonstrates the capacity of robbery to capture the public imagination as one of the more serious and feared of crimes (see Kershaw *et al*, 2001).

The official record reveals little about the nature of robbery in England and Wales. As with many other non-fatal violent offences, data on the key characteristics of personal robbery, such as for victims or their attackers, are limited (Simmons, 2000). Neither is there a clear appreciation as to how these events unfold. Robbery has changed in recent years: for example, victims have become younger and it is likely that our understanding does not reflect the reality. Most robberies do not involve the use of a weapon, for example, and nor do they involve injury to the victim. This is not to suggest that anxiety about robbery is unjustified, nor can concern about robbery be dismissed as "moral panic." The reported rates of increase (that make up these headlines) reflect real and substantial *incremental* increases in the volume of robbery reported by the public, suggesting that the police and public alike have good reason to be concerned (see Waddington, 1986).

This report examines the nature of robbery in England and Wales, specifically focusing on personal robbery which accounts for the bulk of recorded robbery and almost all of the increase in recent years. The findings presented here are based primarily on data collected from over 2,000 crime reports and witness statements across seven police force areas in England and Wales. The remainder of this chapter sets out the nature of the research, the structure of this report and definitional issues around robbery.

Definitions of robbery

In English law, robbery is legally defined under the Theft Act 1968 as follows:

> "A person is guilty of robbery if he steals, and immediately before or at the time of doing so, and in order to do so, he uses force on any person, or puts or seeks to put any person in fear of being then and there subjected to force." Section 8(1).

This legal classification offers the most prescriptive definition, but other terms such as street robbery, street crime or muggings are often considered to be synonymous with robbery. However, these terms differ in their application (Stockdale and Gresham, 1998).

'Street robbery' is often used by police forces (and particularly the Metropolitan Police Service) to describe the offences of robbery, attempted robbery and snatch theft from the person irrespective of location. "Snatch thefts" refer to those incidents where an offender snatches property away from the victim, the force being applied to the property as opposed to the person, and the victim being immediately aware of what has happened. The term 'mugging' originates from the United States and was imported in the 1970s as rising crime became a political issue (Hall *et al* 1978). 'Mugging' has been used as an alternative to street robbery or simply as another term for personal robbery (with or without including snatch thefts). More recently, 'mugging' has been employed in the violence typology used by the British Crime Survey (BCS). 'Street crime' is also used interchangeably with street robbery. It is the term most favoured by the media, but is also used by many North American criminologists to describe non-domestic violent crime in general (Maguire, 1996). In addition to personal robbery and theft snatches, some definitions of street crime encompass a much wider range of offences including pickpocketing, prostitution, drug dealing, wounding, assaults and public order offences (Stockdale and Gresham, 1998). Although the prevailing viewpoint may class all these offences as part of the same problem – particularly snatch thefts and personal robbery – this analysis is concerned only with the 'official' legal classification of robbery as this offers a common definition across all police forces in England and Wales.

Since 1998, the Home Office has counted robbery in two ways: personal and business. Personal robbery is defined under the Home Office counting rules as a robbery "where the goods stolen belong to an individual or group of individuals, rather than a corporate body, regardless of the location of the property, or whether the personal property actually belongs to the person being robbed."[1] This report focuses primarily on personal robbery, though

---

1. According to the counting rules, goods that are the property of business but would generally be regarded as personal property, should be treated as personal property if robbed from the person. Examples of such items are mobile phones, laptop computers and pagers.

some use is briefly made of the official data on all robberies (which include business robberies) in the following chapter to describe recent trends and to set the findings of the research into some context.

Data and methodology

Data have been collected for this study from almost 2,000 crime reports and witness statements for robbery. The key characteristics of the victims and offenders were recorded, along with details of how the robbery occurred, and what property was taken from the victim. This information was collected from seven force basic command units (BCUs). These were Westminster, Lambeth, Bristol and Birmingham city centres, and Stockport and Western and Central Divisions in Lancashire Constabulary (which principally cover offences occurring in Blackpool and Preston respectively). In addition, robberies in two British Transport force areas were also analysed, these being London Underground and London South (which cover the railways of the South East of England).

The sample was taken from a wide range of BCUs with different levels of recorded robbery. The sample may not be representative as such, but by focusing on BCUs in different areas with different levels of recorded robbery, the study aims to capture something of the diversity of the problem. Two samples were taken from Lambeth, the first in February and the second in July. This was primarily as a means of testing whether there were significant seasonal variations between these two 'sweeps'. The two British Transport Police areas (covering the London Underground and railways of the South East) are included because crime on public transport has been the focus of public concern and because previous research has shown links between robbery and transportation routes (Smith and Clarke, 2000; Webb and Laycock, 1991). The research aimed to obtain a sufficiently large sample of robbery cases in each of these BCUs to gain an impression of the nature and complexity of the robbery problem in different areas of England and Wales. Details of all recorded cases of robbery occurring within a specific time period in each area were collected (Table 1.1).

Table 1.1: Research sites and sample period

BCU/ Force Area	Time Period		Number of Robberies
Westminster	January	One month	202
Lambeth	February	15 days	247
Lambeth	July	15 days	245
London Underground	January – March	Three months	126
London South – railways	January – February	Two months	168
Birmingham City Centre	January – February	Two months	193
Bristol City Centre	January – March	Three months	388
Stockport	January – March	Three months	180
Preston (Central Lancs.)	January – May	Four months	112
Blackpool (Western Lancs.)	January – May	Four months	155

Information was gathered on a total of 2,016 crime reports for robbery, of which 1,877 were for personal robbery.[2] The data collected on these personal robberies included 2,065 victims and 4,251 suspects. Of the 1,877 personal robberies recorded, sufficient detail was available to determine the circumstances of how the robbery occurred in 1,721 offences.[3] The following points need to be highlighted when interpreting the data:

- The samples varied in size, as did the time scale over which the data were collected.

- The BCU findings are based on police data and, unlike large-scale victimisation surveys, may not capture the true level of victimisation. The British Crime Survey estimates that only 45 per cent of robberies were recorded by the police in 2001/2 (Simmons et al, 2002).

- Victim details are almost exclusively provided by the victim themselves. However, suspect characteristics are based largely on the accounts of victims and witnesses. Information on ethnicity, for instance, refers to the visible or perceived ethnicity of the suspect as described by the victim, and the age of the suspect is similarly based on the victim's account in line with many other victimisation surveys.

---

2. Only reports for offences of robbery were examined. Theft from the person snatches were not included in the analysis, though there is undoubtedly some linkage between the two. As will be shown in Chapter 4, 14 per cent of personal robberies began as snatch thefts.
3. This difference is largely explained by 145 cases sampled in Bristol where only information on the suspect and victim characteristics were available but not enough to undertake the analysis detailed in Chapter 4 on the nature of robbery.

- The information collected on suspects does not necessarily relate to different offenders. Some prolific offenders may have committed a number of different offences, and they may therefore be double counted. The data do not allow it to be stated that x per cent of robbers have a particular characteristic, only that y per cent of robberies are committed by offenders who appear to have that characteristic.

- These data represent a snapshot of robbery offending in the areas studied. It is not sensible to extrapolate on the basis of these data to give an accurate picture of the overall pattern nationally.

Structure of the report

The remainder of this report is divided into three main sections. Chapter 2 briefly reviews current research, and draws on official data to identify the main trends in recorded robbery in England and Wales in recent years. It also examines its concentration in a small number of metropolitan forces and, within these forces, a small number of BCUs. Some limited comparisons are also made with levels of recorded robbery in other countries. Chapters 3 and 4 draw almost exclusively on the data collected from the BCUs. Chapter 3 describes the main characteristics of victims and offenders in personal robbery, and looks at the changing nature of personal robbery in recent years. Chapter 4 examines in greater detail the circumstances by which personal robbery unfolds and, in particular, the manner by which victims are targeted by their attackers. Chapter 5 summarises the main findings and includes several recommendations.

2   Overview of robbery in England and Wales

Previous research

Most research into robbery in England and Wales has focused on its reduction in commercial premises, and on the motivations of those involved. By comparison, there has been little research into personal robbery or street crime. Studies have focused on the effectiveness of particular robbery reduction initiatives, and offered only rudimentary analysis based on overall crime figures (Stockdale and Gresham, 1998; Webb and Laycock, 1991). The Metropolitan Police Authority publishes regular but brief reports on street crime trends on their website along with details of initiatives being undertaken to target these offences.[4] These reports have generally noted the involvement of young persons aged 14 to 17 years as victims and offenders, though there are variations between different London Boroughs and some areas suffer disproportionately. The theft of mobile phones is cited as a growing problem and this is a trend confirmed by recently published Home Office research (Harrington and Mayhew, 2001).

The British Crime Survey routinely collects information on 'muggings', which includes personal robberies and snatch thefts. The latest BCS estimates that there were 441,000 muggings including 362,000 robberies (Simmons *et al*, 2002).[5] This is a far higher figure than reported to or recorded by the police.[6] This discrepancy may be explained by the possibility that victims did not regard what had happened as serious enough to report to the police or because the victims decided to deal with the matter themselves.[7] Commenting on the rise in reported robbery incidents in 1999, the 2000 BCS observed that although some incidents meet the criterion for robbery, they might be viewed as nearer to bullying incidents. These incidents primarily involved 16 year-olds (the youngest age of victims interviewed by the BCS) and are said to have had a marked impact on robbery trends (Kershaw *et al*, 2001).

---

4.   The website address for the Metropolitan Police Authority is http://www.mpa.gov.uk.
5.   Based on best estimate; lower estimates suggest 363,000 muggings and 288,000 robberies and higher estimates suggest 519,000 and 436,000 offences respectively (Simmons et al, 2002).
6.   The small number of offences captured in the survey means that these estimates contain within them potentially large statistical variation.
7.   These are the two most frequently cited reasons for victims not reporting crimes recorded by the BCS under its violence typology, which include muggings and the offence of robbery. Other reasons include fear of reprisal, the incident being reported to authorities other than the police, the inconvenience of reporting and a reluctance to make contact with the police (Simmons et al, 2002)

Mugging has consistently been regarded as a serious crime, as illustrated in the most recent BCS (Simmons *et al*, 2002). The number of persons worried about mugging has remained fairly constant, but is higher in inner city areas – as with most crime. Older persons feel more at risk, despite the fact that risks are far higher for younger persons. The majority of muggings were carried out by more than one offender, echoing another study by Barker *et al*, (1993). One of the most curious findings from the BCS, however, is that in one in five robberies the victim knew the offender well, and in a further 14 per cent knew the offender by sight (Kershaw *et al*, 2001). This finding was not replicated in this study, which found that only 5 per cent of victims reported that they knew the identity of the suspect. While this shows the advantages of victimisation studies, the BCS can only help provide a partial picture of the robbery problem. Firstly, the BCS only interviews those over the age of 16 living in private households, and this is problematic since many robbery victims are now known to be below this age. Secondly, and despite the large sample sizes of the BCS, the findings on robbery or 'mugging' involve relatively small numbers of victims, and are unlikely to reflect the concentration of robbery within primarily urban areas. Consequently, while the BCS gives a flavour of what the nature of robbery might be, it is not as yet a reliable measure of trends and patterns in this particular offence.

The only recent detailed analysis on the nature of robbery in this country involved a study of personal robbery and snatch thefts undertaken by Barker *et al*, (1993). The study provided some insight into how these robberies and snatch thefts occurred. Many victims of robbery were threatened with violence prior to handing over property, but in some cases violence was used on them without provocation and then the property was removed. In some snatch offences, victims were at first approached with some innocuous request to set the victim off guard, such as asking for the time of day, while in other cases they were approached from behind and caught unawares as the suspect grabbed the property from the victim.

The study found that female victims predominated accounting for 57 per cent of victims, half of all victims were under the age of 25, with 9 per cent aged under 16 years. Group offending was common for robbery, but not for snatch thefts. Over one in ten victims were coming from or going to a public transport location such as a bus stop or underground station at the time of the robbery. Violence was used in 44 per cent of cases with victims sustaining injury in 28 per cent of cases. Weapons were present in one in five cases, but rarely were they actually used on the victim (e.g. stabbed). In many cases the victim had more than one type of property taken, but the main source of immediate gain for the offender was cash. Many items taken from victims were on display at the time, in particular handbags and jewellery, or personal stereos in some cases of bullying related robberies. While providing a valuable insight into personal robbery, Barker *et al* 's analysis was based on offences committed in 1987, and the nature of these offences may have changed as recorded robbery continues to increase.

Recent trends in recorded robbery

Figure 2.1: Recorded robbery in England and Wales, 1990 – 2001/02*

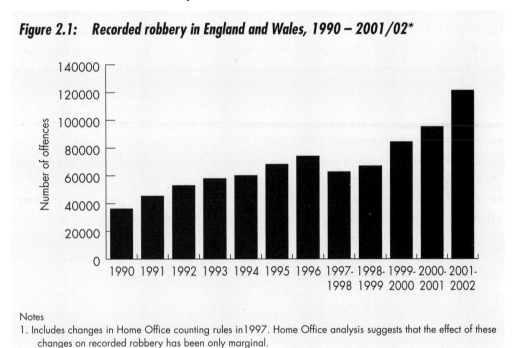

Notes
1. Includes changes in Home Office counting rules in1997. Home Office analysis suggests that the effect of these changes on recorded robbery has been only marginal.

Offences recorded as robbery (personal and business) by the police in England and Wales have more than doubled over the last ten years. Some of the largest increases, in terms of volume, have been in recent years (Figure 2.1). Between April 2001 and March 2002, robbery increased by 28 per cent, or 26,221 offences (Simmons *et al*, 2002). This followed a 13 per cent rise the previous year, and a 26 per cent increase the year before that (an increase of 10,877 and 17,441 offences respectively).

Personal robbery accounts for the bulk of recorded robbery in England and Wales. Between April 2001 and March 2002, personal robbery accounted for 89 per cent of all robbery, and almost all of the increase. Personal robbery continues to increase at a faster rate than business robbery. Business robbery increased by 6 per cent in 2001/02 compared to the previous year, while personal robbery increased by 31 per cent.

Geographic concentration

Robbery is concentrated in relatively few police force areas, and predominately in urban metropolitan forces. This is the case to some extent with all recorded crime, but particularly so with robbery. The ten police forces currently part of the Street Crime Initiative accounted for 83 per cent of all recorded robbery between April 2001 and March 2002 (Figure 2.2).

Figure 2.2: **Recorded robbery in ten SCI forces, April 2001 to March 2002**

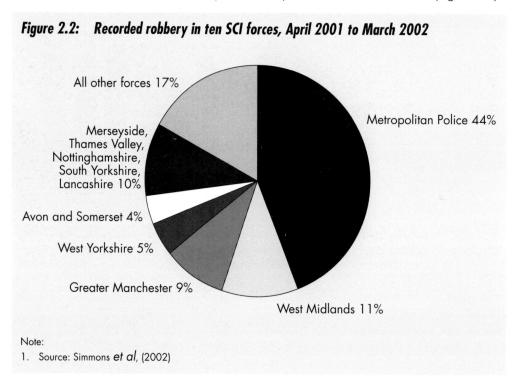

All other forces 17%

Merseyside,
Thames Valley,
Nottinghamshire,
South Yorkshire,
Lancashire 10%

Avon and Somerset 4%

West Yorkshire 5%

Greater Manchester 9%

Metropolitan Police 44%

West Midlands 11%

Note:
1. Source: Simmons *et al*, (2002)

The Metropolitan Police Service dominates this picture, accounting for 44 per cent of all recorded robbery in England and Wales. While this is disproportionately high when compared to other crime types, the predominance of robbery in the Metropolitan Police Service appears to have declined in recent years. In 1987, 55 per cent of all recorded robbery occurred within the Metropolitan Police Service (Barker *et al*, 1993).

Recorded robbery by Basic Command Unit

An analysis of recorded robbery (personal and business) by BCU suggests that within forces the pattern of robbery is further concentrated. In fact, robbery is disproportionately concentrated in a smaller number of primarily urban BCUs when compared to other crime types such as burglary and violent crime in general (Figure 2.3).

Figure 2.3: **Recorded crime April 2001 to March 2002 ranked by BCU: robbery, violent crime and burglary dwelling**

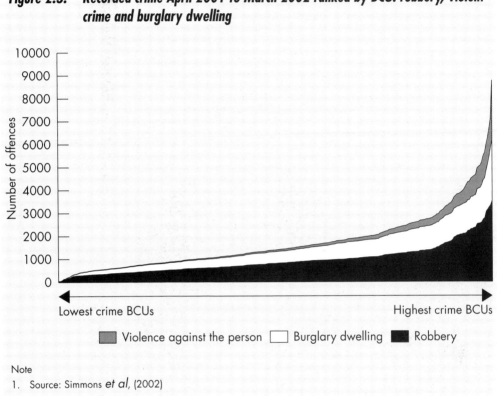

Note
1. Source: Simmons *et al*, (2002)

The 20 highest BCUs for each of these crime types accounted for 19 per cent of recorded burglary, and 20 per cent of all violent crime. By contrast, the 20 highest BCUs accounted for 42 per cent of all recorded robbery. Put another way, just 7 per cent of BCUs in England and Wales accounted for two in every five recorded robberies between April 2001 and March 2002.

The 20 highest robbery BCUs cover five force areas. Fifteen are located in the Metropolitan Police Service, two in Greater Manchester, and one each in the West Midlands, Avon and Somerset and Nottinghamshire respectively (Table 2.1). These BCU level data suggest that robbery is a distinctly urban crime.

Table 2.1: Recorded robbery in England and Wales April 2001 to March 2002: twenty highest BCUs

Basic Command Unit	Police force	Robbery, offences recorded 01/02	Robbery as % of all robbery in England and Wales
Lambeth	Metropolitan	6,465	5.3
Southwark	Metropolitan	3,086	2.5
Hackney	Metropolitan	3,009	2.5
South Manchester	Greater Manchester	2,850	2.3
Central Bristol	Avon & Somerset	2,806	2.3
City of Westminster	Metropolitan	2,763	2.3
Haringey	Metropolitan	2,626	2.2
Camden	Metropolitan	2,439	2.0
Newham	Metropolitan	2,400	2.0
Brent	Metropolitan	2,359	1.9
Ealing	Metropolitan	2,264	1.9
Waltham Forest	Metropolitan	2,154	1.8
Tower Hamlets	Metropolitan	2,117	1.7
Croydon	Metropolitan	2,095	1.7
Nottingham	Nottinghamshire	1,984	1.6
Lewisham	Metropolitan	1,966	1.6
Wandsworth	Metropolitan	1,948	1.6
North Manchester	Greater Manchester	1,901	1.6
Islington	Metropolitan	1,659	1.4
Birmingham City Centre	West Midlands	1,451	1.2
	Total 20 BCUs	50,342	41.5
	Total England and Wales	*121,375*	*100.0*

Notes:
1. Source: Simmons et. al. (2002)
2. These twenty highest robbery BCUs are grouped in two BCU families'. Overall England and Wales has 280 BCUs grouped into fourteen 'families.'
3. There is likely to be some variation between forces on the extent to which allegations are eventually recorded as a crime (Burrows *et al* 2000).

International comparisons

Making comparisons of recorded crime between different jurisdictions can be complicated (Barclay and Tavares, 2002). With robbery, there appears to be broad agreement on the definition (namely the taking of property with threats or with force), though some classifications encompass a wider range of offence types but which are small in number (such as blackmail, for instance). These are unlikely to have a marked impact on the overall level of robbery. Recording practices may have more of an impact, however, though to what extent is difficult to estimate.[8] With these caveats in mind, the level of recorded robbery in England and Wales, measured here in crimes per 100,000 of the population, has been compared with those of other countries for the period 1996-2000 (the latest year for which 'comparable' information was available): the United States, France, Germany, Canada, Australia and Scotland. Figure 2.4 displays this information on rates of recorded robbery for these seven jurisdictions.

Figure 2.4: Recorded robbery per 100,000 of national population

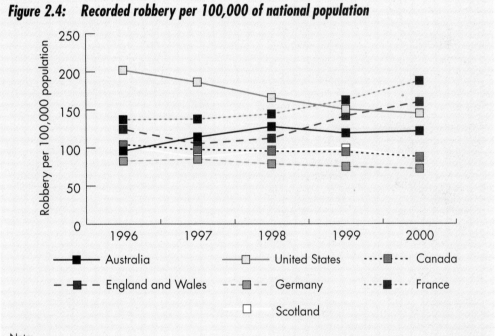

Note:
1. Sources: Bureau of Crime Statistics and Research, New South Wales (Australia); Federal Bureau of Investigation, Uniform Crime Reports, Index of Crime (United States); Statistics Canada; Home Office (England and Wales); Scottish Office (Scotland); Interpol, International Crime Statistics (France, Germany).
2. Comparisons are for offences classified as robbery, though some countries use the category 'robbery and violent theft.'

Of the seven jurisdictions, France had the highest level of robbery per 100,000 population in 2000 and increases have largely mirrored those in England and Wales, which has the second highest robbery level in this comparison (Figure 2.4). England and Wales have

---

8.   The recorded crime levels for robbery will be affected by many factors including: different legal and criminal justice systems; rates at which crimes are reported to the police and recorded by them; differences in the point at which crime is measured and differences in the rules by which multiple offences are counted (Barclay et al, 2000).

overtaken the United States in recent years and now have a higher level of robbery per 100,000 population. The United States has seen a 28 per cent reduction in robbery since 1996 and a 47 per cent reduction since 1990.[9] Recorded robbery in Canada is also in decline, and has levelled in Australia since 1998. Scotland provides the most appropriate comparison with England and Wales. The number of robberies per 100,000 population is lower in Scotland than in England and Wales and this difference has become more marked since 1998. There were 86 recorded robberies per 100,000 population in Scotland in 2000 compared to 160 in England and Wales. Recorded robbery in Scotland fell by 13 per cent between 1999 and 2000.

9.   Federal Bureau of Investigation, Uniform Crime Reports.

3   Personal robbery: characteristics of suspects and victims

This chapter examines the characteristics of the victims of personal robbery and those of their attackers. This information is critical to aiding our understanding of the nature of personal robbery and, ultimately, how these events unfold. The key areas of age, gender, and ethnicity are examined here, supplemented by other information including the victim's employment status, aspects of group offending, and the time and location of offences. The data are taken primarily from the BCU analysis, although this also includes some trend analysis using data obtained from the Metropolitan Police Service.

Gender of victims and suspects

Personal robbery is a predominately male crime. Overall, three-quarters of victims (76%) and nine out of ten suspects (94%) were male (Table 3.1). Seven out of ten (71%) personal robberies involved male victims being attacked by male suspects and one in five (21%) involved female victims being attacked by male suspects.

Table 3.1:   Gender of victim and suspect by BCU/ BTP area

				Row percentages
	Victim		Suspect	
	Male	Female	Male	Female
	%	%	%	%
Bristol City Centre	78	22	96	4
Birmingham City Centre	80	20	93	7
Westminster	77	23	92	8
Stockport	82	18	92	8
Lambeth – February	56	44	93	7
Lambeth- July	68	32	96	4
Preston	81	19	90	10
Blackpool	72	28	92	8
London Underground	93	7	97	3
BTP-London South	84	16	95	5
All BCUs	76	24	94	6
Total N	1563	495	3802	247

Notes:
1. N = 2058 (victims), 4049 (suspects); Missing data = 7 (victims), 192 (suspects).
2. Suspect data based on victim's description of their attacker

There were some marked variations between the BCUs for victims. Lambeth had the lowest proportion of male victims (56% and 68% in the February and July samples respectively). This difference suggests that there may be seasonal differences in the nature of robbery within BCUs. In contrast, victims of personal robbery on the London Underground were almost exclusively male (93%). These differences are set out in Table 3.1. The picture for suspects was more stable, with little variation between BCUs.

Female offending in personal robbery is relatively rare, accounting for only 6 per cent of all suspects. Most females co-offend with other males (60% of female offenders), which means that only 3 per cent of personal robberies involved either a female acting alone or with other females (Figure 3.1).

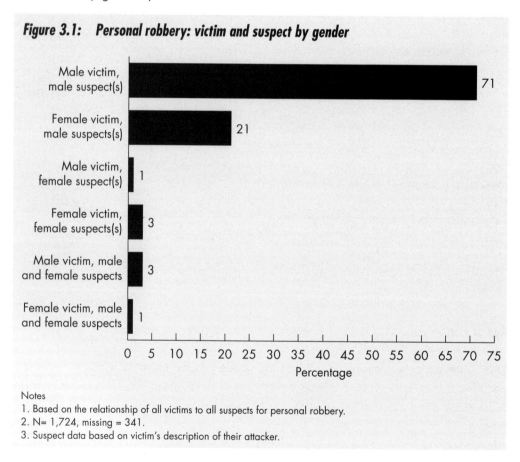

Figure 3.1: Personal robbery: victim and suspect by gender

Notes
1. Based on the relationship of all victims to all suspects for personal robbery.
2. N= 1,724, missing = 341.
3. Suspect data based on victim's description of their attacker.

Offending in groups

Robbery committed by two or more persons is the norm in personal robbery. Over six out of ten personal robberies involved two or more offenders acting together (Table 3.2). Robberies involving younger victims aged 20 years and under were more likely to involve two or more offenders (71% did) than robberies involving victims aged 21 years and over (56%). Robberies against male victims involved group offending on seven out of ten occasions (70%), while robberies involving female victims were mostly committed by an offender acting alone (59%). It follows that offending in groups of two or more was higher in those BCUs with the largest proportion of victims aged 20 years and under.

Table 3.2:   Personal robberies involving group offending

Row Percentages

| Characteristic of victims | Number of suspects | | | | | Total multiple offending | Total victims % |
	One	Two	Three	Four	More than five		
20 years and under	30	33	17	9	12	71	100
21 years and over	44	32	13	4	6	56	100
Male victims	31	35	17	7	10	70	100
Female victims	59	25	9	4	4	41	100
All victims	38	33	15	6	8	62	100
Total all offences	645	552	252	104	146	1054	1699

Notes
1. Based on the total number of personal robberies
2. N= 1699, missing = 28

Age of victims and suspects

One of the distinctive features about personal robbery is the extent to which victimisation and offending is increasingly concentrated in younger age groups. The data collected from BCUs show that a large proportion of victims and the majority of offenders were aged between 11 and 20 years of age (Figure 3.2).[10] This was particularly the case for offenders

10. Information on the suspect's age is based on the victim's recollection as described in crime reports or witness statements. The victim provided details of the suspect's age in 80 per cent of cases. Research on the accuracy of eyewitness testimony suggests that witnesses are generally most accurate when they are estimating the age of someone of a similar age to themselves since they will be more familiar with that age group (Kebbell and Wagstaff, 1999). This would suggest that the BCU data on victim descriptions of their attackers' age would generally be accurate since most victims were targeted by suspects from a similar age group.

with seven out of ten described by the victim as being in this age group, with just over half of all offenders assessed as aged between 16 and 20 years of age. Figure 3.2 shows that offending by those over the age of 25 was relatively rare. Police data on persons charged with an offence of robbery support the general observation that offending is concentrated amongst those under the age of 20 years (see below).

Victimisation was less concentrated in the 11-20 age group when compared to offenders, though personal robbery was likely to affect this age group more than any other. Just over one in five (22%) personal robberies involved victims aged between 11-15 years, with a similar proportion (23%) aged between 16-20 years. The age profile tails off more gradually for victims than that for suspects, reflecting the finding that there is a significant minority of older victims being offended against by younger persons (Figure 3.2). Two out of every five (42%) personal robberies involved a victim and a suspect under the age of 21 years (Figure 3.3).

Figure 3.2: Age of victim and suspect for personal robbery

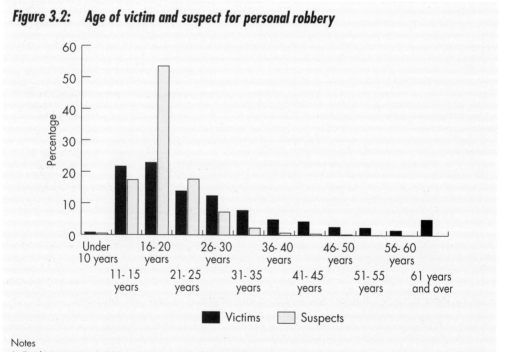

Notes
1. Total N victims = 2,254, missing = 112; suspects = 3,410, missing = 831.
2. Age of victim as recorded in crime report or witness statement. Suspect age based on victim's description of their attacker(s) as recorded in crime report or witness statement.

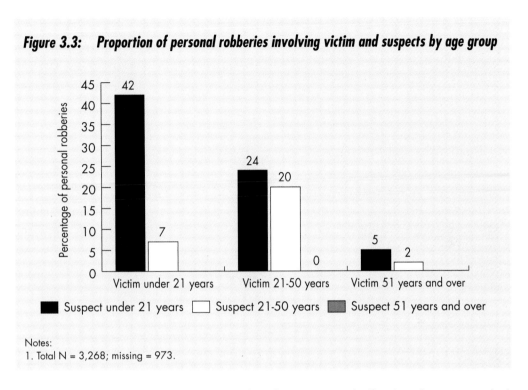

Figure 3.3:   Proportion of personal robberies involving victim and suspects by age group

Notes:
1. Total N = 3,268; missing = 973.

This generalised overview of the age profiles for victims and offenders disguises marked variations between the BCUs sampled (Table 3.3). Victims were typically younger in Stockport, Birmingham and the London Underground. By contrast, victims were more likely to be older in Westminster, Bristol, Lambeth and Blackpool. Blackpool had the largest proportion of elderly victims aged 61 years and over (15%). Although Lambeth was the BCU with the highest level of recorded robbery in England and Wales in 2001/02, it had the smallest proportion of victims in either the 11-15 or the 16-20 age groups of any of the BCUs sampled.

These differences are likely to reflect, in part, the differing age structure of the local resident population (the potential available victims) in each area. For example, it would appear that those aged under 16 and living in Stockport are much more likely to be victims of personal robbery than those of similar age living in Birmingham, where the proportion of victims under 16 years is almost equal to that found in the resident population. Similarly, over a quarter of the resident population of Blackpool are over the age of 60 years, and this may partly explain why a significantly higher proportion of victims of robbery are in this age group when compared to other BCUs.[11] Local population movements at different times of the

---

11.   In Stockport, 20 per cent of the population is estimated to be under the age of 16 years, and 23 per cent in Birmingham. The proportion of victims in this age group for these two areas was 46 per cent and 24 per cent respectively. In Blackpool, 26 per cent of the population are estimated to be over 60 years, and 15.4 per cent of all robbery victims were in this age group. These figures are derived from 1991 Census estimates (neighbourhood statistics): http://www.statistics.gov.uk/neighbourhood

day caused by aspects of everyday activity (e.g. children travelling to school in neighbouring areas, people travelling to entertainment districts in city centres), will also impact on the opportunities for robbery. This further illustrates the point that patterns in robbery victimisation are dependent on local population conditions.

Female victims tend to be older than male victims. Table 3.3 shows that female victimisation peaked in the 21-25 and 26-30 age groups, with each age group accounting for 17 per cent of female victims. There is evidence to suggest that of the elderly, women rather than men, were more likely to be victims. This broadly accords with a separate study of police data, reported in Povey et al, (2001), which found that 15 per cent of female victims of robbery were aged 70 or over. In this study, victims over the age of 61 years accounted for 14 per cent of all female victims, compared to just 2 per cent of male victims. Female suspects, by contrast, were typically younger than male suspects (Table 3.4). Over a third (34%) of female suspects were aged 11-15 years compared to 16 per cent of male suspects. That said, female suspects in personal robbery were few in number, and most female suspects co-offended with male suspects.

Offender age profiles also differed between the BCUs, though not as much as victim age profiles (Table 3.4). Offenders were more likely to be older in Bristol, Birmingham and Blackpool and younger in Stockport, the London Underground and the railways. However, in all BCUs the offender was most frequently estimated by the victim to be 16-20 years, (Table 3.4).

Change in age of suspect and victims over time

This overall picture for the age profiles of victims and suspects is not static. Data obtained from the Metropolitan Police Service suggest that robbery has changed markedly as victims and offenders have become typically younger and greater in number. Moreover, the increasingly younger age profile for robbery offences is not matched for other offence types, such as violence against the person or burglary.

Over the last ten years there has been a pronounced shift towards the victimisation of younger age groups. Metropolitan Police Service data on personal robbery show that the number of 11-15 and 16-20 year-old victims has increased threefold (by 320% and 296% respectively) since 1993 (Figure 3.4). Overall, the number of victims increased by 121 per cent during this period. These increases have been most dramatic since 1998. One in four of all victims in the Metropolitan Police Service are now aged between 11 and 15 years; 16 to 20 year-olds now account for 22 per cent of all victims. By contrast, in 1993 these two age groups accounted for 12 per cent and 13 per cent of all victims respectively.

Table 3.3: **Age of victim by BCU/ BTP force area, and by sex of victim**

Row percentages

	Age of victim											
	Under 10	11-15	16- 20	21-25	26-30	31-35	36-40	41-45	46-50	51-55	56-60	61 & over
Bristol City Centre	0	13	25	20	12	7	5	5	4	3	1	5
Birmingham City Centre	1	23	29	12	11	4	4	3	3	2	3	4
Westminster	-	13	28	19	14	11	4	3	1	3	1	4
Stockport	1	45	26	5	7	3	2	3	1	1	1	5
Lambeth – February	0	13	14	14	20	13	5	4	3	4	3	5
Lambeth- July	2	11	12	17	17	14	8	6	4	2	1	6
Preston	-	21	28	11	11	4	6	6	3	2	2	7
Blackpool	1	22	11	10	11	4	8	8	4	3	1	15
London Underground	1	38	28	14	7	6	2	2	2	-	-	-
London South - railway	1	43	36	4	5	3	3	2	1	2	1	-
Male victims	1	25	26	13	11	7	5	4	2	2	1	2
Female victims	0	10	13	17	17	9	6	5	4	4	2	14
All BCUs	1	22	23	14	12	8	5	4	3	2	1	5
Total N victims	13	431	455	276	246	155	97	85	52	48	29	100

Notes:
1. N = 1987, missing = 90

Table 3.4: Age of suspect by BCU/ BTP force area, and by sex of suspect

Row percentages

	Under 10	11-15	16- 20	21-25	26-30	31-35	36-40	41-45	46-50	51-55	56-60	61 & over
						Age of suspect						
Bristol City Centre	0	10	38	31	16	3	0	1	-	-	0	-
Birmingham City Centre	1	26	35	29	6	2	1	1	-	-	-	-
Westminster	0	12	57	18	8	2	-	1	1	0	-	-
Stockport	-	21	71	6	2	-	0	0	1	-	-	-
Lambeth – February	-	24	41	16	9	5	3	0	1	-	-	-
Lambeth- July	1	14	54	18	8	3	1	0	-	-	-	-
Preston	-	11	65	17	6	1	-	1	-	-	-	-
Blackpool	1	18	40	22	13	7	0	-	-	-	-	-
London Underground	-	17	65	14	2	0	0	-	0	-	-	-
London South - railway	0	21	71	6	2	0	-	-	-	-	-	-
Male suspects	0	16	54	18	7	2	1	0	0	-	-	-
Female suspects	0	34	41	14	6	2	1	1	-	-	-	-
All BCUs	0	17	54	18	7	2	1	0	0	0	0	0
Total N suspects	14	595	1825	603	248	76	24	15	8	1	1	0

Notes:
1. N = 3410, missing = 831
2. Suspect information based on the account of the victim

Figure 3.4: **Percentage change in age of victim since 1993: personal robbery in the Metropolitan Police Service**

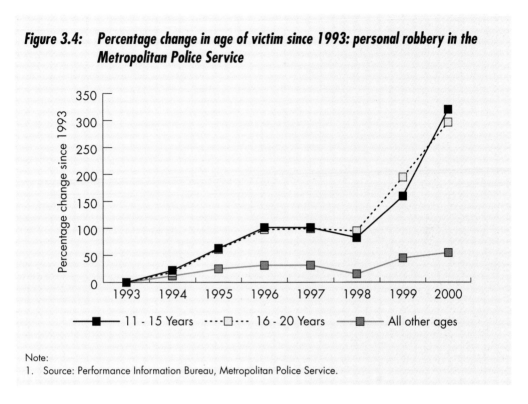

Note:
1. Source: Performance Information Bureau, Metropolitan Police Service.

The age of suspects for personal robbery also appears to have shifted dramatically to younger age groups during this same period. This finding is derived from police data on persons charged with robbery (personal) in the Metropolitan Police Service over the same period. This shows that the 11-20 age group accounted for 78 per cent of all offenders in 2000, compared to 56 per cent in 1993. Much of this change can be attributed to the growth of offenders aged 11-15 years, which accounted for 36 per cent of suspects charged in 2000 compared to 15 per cent in 1993. The number of 11-15 year-olds charged with an offence of personal robbery has increased fivefold (by 483%) since 1993 (Figure 3.5). The latest year (2000) witnessed the largest increase in the number of 11-15 year-olds charged with personal robbery.

Figure 3.5: Percentage change in suspects charged with personal robbery in the Metropolitan Police Service since 1993

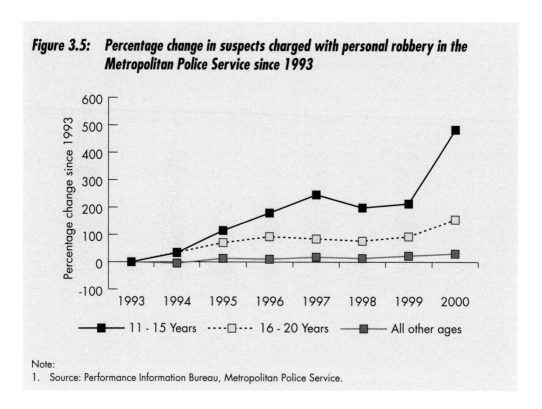

Note:
1. Source: Performance Information Bureau, Metropolitan Police Service.

The younger age profile for robbery offences is not matched for other offence types, such as violence against the person or burglary. Figure 3.6 shows the ages of suspects charged with offences of robbery (personal), violence against the person and burglary of a dwelling by the Metropolitan Police for the year 2001. Those charged with offences of burglary dwelling and violence against the person were typically older than those charged with robbery. Only 13 per cent of those charged with robbery were aged between 21-30 years compared to 35 per cent and 30 per cent of those charged with burglary and violence against the person. Conversely, only 8 per cent of those charged with robbery were aged over 31 years compared to 32 per cent and 40 per cent respectively for burglary and violence against the person.

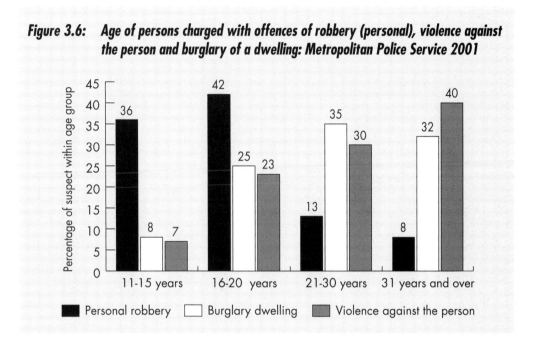

Figure 3.6: *Age of persons charged with offences of robbery (personal), violence against the person and burglary of a dwelling: Metropolitan Police Service 2001*

Ethnicity and personal robbery

Data on the ethnicity of victims and suspects were collated from the police crime reports. For suspects, ethnicity was based on victims' descriptions of their attacker given in the crime report or in their witness statements. Ethnicity and street crime could easily become a highly emotive issue and for this reason data needs to be handled with special care. Before commenting on the findings, the following points need to be taken into account when interpreting this BCU level data on ethnicity:

- The data presented simply tell us about the characteristics of offenders involved in the sample of robberies studied. They cannot reveal anything about the ethnic profile of the offender population since a small number of prolific offenders may be responsible for a large number of offences.

- Variations in ethnicity within the offence data presented will to some extent reflect the ethnic make-up of the local population. It is not sensible to aggregate these data and extrapolate the findings to create a national picture. The data have been taken from a handful of BCUs which will not be representative.

Table 3.5:   Ethnicity of victim and suspect by BCU/ BTP force area.

Row percentages

	Suspects				Victims			
	White	Black	Asian	Other	White	Black	Asian	Other
Bristol City Centre	34	58	4	4	92	5	3	-
Birmingham City Centre	11	64	22	3	85	13	2	-
Westminster	29	62	2	7	67	11	11	11
Stockport	73	7	5	15	98	1	1	-
Lambeth – February	10	86	1	4	79	12	7	2
Lambeth- July	9	87	1	3	77	16	5	2
Preston	77	5	15	2	95	-	4	1
Blackpool	99	1	0	-	99	1	-	-
London Underground	11	82	4	3	73	4	21	2
Railway- London South	26	70	2	2	91	4	4	-

Notes:
1. Suspect N= 4241; victim N = 1910, missing = 167
2. Suspect information based on best source of information: offender identified else victim's recollection as recorded in crime reports and witness statements
3. There were differences in coding of ethnicity, with some forces and BCUs using four or five categories and others six. For present purposes, White includes White and Dark European; Black is Afro-Caribbean and 'black'; Asians are those from the Indian Sub- Continent; and 'Other' includes those ethnic groups not represented, for example Arabian, Egyptian, Chinese, Japanese, and those of mixed origin (which includes those described in witness statements and crime reports as 'half-caste').

- It has been traditional to compare data about the ethnic make-up of offenders or victims with the ethnic make-up of the local resident population. Whilst we do so here – because we have no other available denominator – there are reasons why this can be misleading. The 'resident population' takes no account of movement into and out of areas from elsewhere – especially city centre areas where robbery in particular is concentrating. Nor is 'resident population' necessarily an accurate guide to who actually spends time regularly on the streets. For these reasons comparisons with resident populations may distort the under, or over representation of particular groups.

- Although victims and witnesses are generally accurate at establishing when someone comes from a different racial background to their own (Kebbell and Wagstaff, 1999)[12] these descriptions may not accurately capture differences within groups.[13]

Ethnicity of suspects and victims

Table 3.5 shows the ethnicity of suspects as a proportion of all suspects for each BCU sampled and Table 3.6 provides some estimates of the ethnic make-up of the local population corresponding to each BCU. These population estimates are derived from the Office of National Statistics (ONS) Labour Force Survey (LFS).

Table 3.6: **Ethnicity of local population based on Labour Force Survey estimates**

| Place of residence | % of population by ethnic origin | | | | Total N |
	White	Black	Asian	Other	
Lambeth	57	31	*	9	269,096
Westminster	72	8	9	11	222,427
Birmingham	69	6	20	4	999,313
Bristol City Centre	94	3	*	3	401,640
Stockport	96	*	*	*	289,004
Preston	89	*	8	*	134,359
Blackpool	98	*	*	*	143,685

Notes:
1. Population by ethnic origin as at August 2001
2. Source: ONS Labour Force Survey. LFS is based on a sample size of around 60,000 households. In spite of this large sample size, like any sample survey, estimates from the LFS are subject to sampling error. Population estimates that fall below the threshold of reliability as defined by the ONS are denoted with an asterix and are not detailed.
3. Data on ethnicity not available for equivalent BTP areas

12. However, they are less accurate in describing the specific racial group to which an individual belongs (ibid., 14).
13. For instance, black Somalian as opposed to black Caribbean. Persons of mixed race are similarly inadequately accommodated.

The ethnic make-up of robbery suspects varied markedly between BCUs. In part, these variations reflect differences in the local populations of these areas. Lambeth, for instance, had a high proportion of black suspects (86% and 87% in the February and July sample respectively) (Table 3.5). But it also had the largest resident black population of any of the BCUs sampled – 31 per cent of the resident population is estimated to be black.[14] Black suspects for personal robbery also predominated in nearby Westminster, and in Bristol and Birmingham City Centres (62%, 58% and 64% respectively), though not to the same degree as in Lambeth. In Birmingham City Centre, the proportion of Asian suspects (22%) – while relatively high in comparison to other BCUs sampled – largely mirrored that found in the local population of Birmingham. This was similarly the case in Preston, which was the only other BCU with a significant proportion of Asian suspects (15% of all suspects were described as Asian). It too had a substantial minority Asian population. In three BCUs the majority of suspects were reported to be white (Stockport 73%, Preston 77% and Blackpool 99%), again in part reflecting the local resident population differences.

It would appear, therefore, that visible ethnic minorities are over-represented as offenders in some BCUs but not in others. However, direct comparisons with static local resident population estimates are complicated by the fact that many of the BCUs will have substantial population movements during the day as people commute to work, and in the evening as people travel to bars, clubs and entertainment venues. Neither do these findings take account of those victims who, for various reasons, will not report an offence of robbery to the police.

In all the BCUs sampled, the majority of victims were white and the proportion of black and Asian victims was relatively small (Table 3.5). There was some variation between the BCUs, though not nearly as marked as the ethnicity of suspects. Lambeth, Westminster and Birmingham had higher proportions of black victims (12% and 16% respectively in Lambeth February and July samples, 11% Westminster and 13% Birmingham). The proportion of Asian victims was markedly higher on the London Underground (21% of victims).[15] It is not possible to compare this seemingly high figure with any corresponding population data for the London Underground area. But similar comparisons for the other BCUs sampled would appear to suggest that visible ethnic minorities' reporting robbery to the police are over-represented in relation to the resident population in some BCUs, but again not in others.

---

14. These figures fail to take account of the fact that an even higher proportion of the younger population will be black (Clancy et al, 2001).

15. Research by Clancy et al, (2001) found that minority ethnic persons are more likely to be victims of 'mugging'. There is also evidence to suggest that visible ethnic minorities are reporting being a victim of personal robbery in increasing numbers. Data from the MPS show that the number of black victims has increased disproportionately when compared to victims of other ethnicities. Between 1993 and 2000, the number of black victims reporting a robbery to the police increased by 235 per cent compared to 97 per cent for white victims and 97 per cent for Asian victims. Overall, the number of victims of personal robbery increased by 105 per cent. (Details in Appendix Table A3.1).

While these findings on ethnicity cannot be extrapolated to give any overall picture of the ethnicity of victims and suspects in robbery, they do emphasise the importance of local population differences in explaining the common characteristics of those identified in police crime reports. Finally, it is also important to consider wider socio-economic and demographic factors that will mediate the levels of risk between different ethnic groups. Research suggests that these are more important in determining victim-offender characteristics than ethnicity itself.[16] For example, people from minority ethnic groups are more likely to be younger, to be unemployed and live in inner city areas – all of which increases the risks of victimisation regardless of ethnicity (Clancy et al, 2001).

Employment status of victims

Over 40 per cent of victims were employed at the time of the robbery. School children accounted for 21 per cent of all victims, students 14 per cent, unemployed persons 15 per cent and retired (which included a small number of economically inactive persons), 8 per cent. Comparisons with local population estimates indicate that employed and retired persons are less likely to report a robbery to the police, while unemployed persons are more likely.[17] Given that many victims are under the age of twenty years, it is not surprising that most victims in these younger age categories are either school children or students. Eight out of ten victims aged 20 years and under fall into this category. Only one in ten (11%) of victims in these age groups were employed at the time of the robbery. This compared to 60 per cent of victims over 21 years of age being in employment at the time of the robbery. These differences between the two age groups are shown in Figure 3.7. However, these are important characteristics as they provide some indication of the victim's routine activities that may place them in certain locations at particular times of the day and which may in turn impact on how such victims are targeted by suspects. These issues are explored further in Chapter 4.

---

16. The obvious exception to this rule is racially motivated crime, which is examined in some depth in Clancy et al, (2001).
17. Comparisons are indicative only and there will be disparity between victim defined employment status and that recorded for official purposes. The data are derived from the ONS website (neighbourhood statistics). There is no available data on student populations.

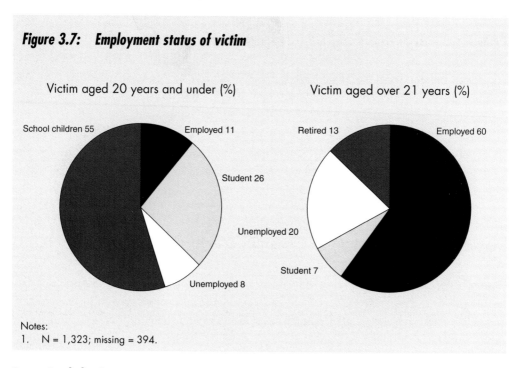

Figure 3.7: Employment status of victim

Victim aged 20 years and under (%)

School children 55   Employed 11

Student 26

Unemployed 20

Unemployed 8

Victim aged over 21 years (%)

Retired 13   Employed 60

Student 7

Notes:
1.   N = 1,323; missing = 394.

Reporting behaviour

Most personal robberies were reported to the police within the hour (62%). However, a sizeable proportion took longer than an hour; 18 per cent took between one and four hours and 16 per cent took more than eight hours to report (Figure 3.8). Of those contacting the police to report a robbery, 45 per cent of personal robberies were reported via a '999' call. A further 7 per cent were reported to passing police patrols. A further 16 per cent of personal robberies were reported to the police via a non-emergency telephone, and 28 per cent were reported at the front desk of the local police station (Figure 3.8).

Figure 3. 8: Reporting characteristics in personal robbery

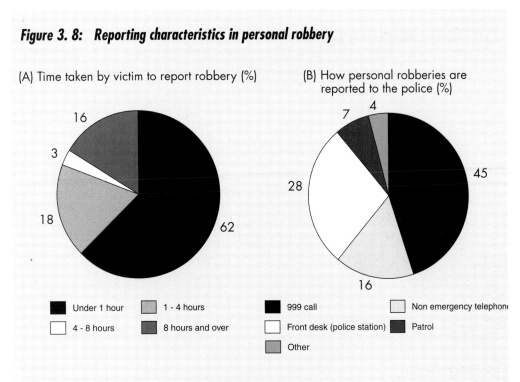

(A) Time taken by victim to report robbery (%)

(B) How personal robberies are reported to the police (%)

■ Under 1 hour	▨ 1 - 4 hours	■ 999 call	□ Non emergency telephon⟨
□ 4 - 8 hours	▨ 8 hours and over	□ Front desk (police station)	■ Patrol
		▨ Other	

Notes:
1. Excludes 4 force areas for which accurate information on victim reporting was not available: Preston, Blackpool, London Underground and London South Railways.
2. (A) N= 1,365; missing = 64. (B) N= 1,153; missing = 49.

These findings are important for a number of reasons. First, given that robbery is a serious offence (and perceived as such by victims), it is perhaps curious that a significant proportion is not reported as soon as the incident has occurred. Second, only '999' emergency calls are likely to receive an immediate response, together with those who manage to locate a passing patrol. Other research, albeit on different crime types, has pointed to the speed of alerting the police as a critical factor in successful detection (Coupe and Griffiths, 1996), and there is evidence that this is just as important for the offence of robbery (Burrows *et al*, 2003). This means that the likelihood of detection will be constrained by the reporting behaviours of victims. It is also curious that a comparatively large number of personal robberies are reported direct to the station at the front desk, and many of these will be late reports. There appear to be a number of reasons for these differences:

● In some of these cases victims will have made their way home before reporting the incident. This may be the case with victims frightened or in shock, or with younger victims who tell their parents about the incident on their return home.

Victims of robberies that occurred at night may prefer to wait until the morning to report the incident (sometimes because they are intoxicated through alcohol). Late reports are more likely to relate to offences that occurred in the evening time, and at night.

- The nature of the sample – focused on predominately urban BCUs – may account for a relatively high number of front desk reports. Victims may simply find it easier to report at the front desk of a local police station. However, this is not true for all victims, and it would appear that some victims' characteristics are related to reporting behaviours. For instance, retired victims were more likely to report the offence via an emergency '999' call, students and unemployed persons were more likely to report at the front desk (see Figure A3.1). The reasons for this are not clear from this research, although this is clearly an area worthy of further investigation.

- Robberies involving mobile phones were more likely to involve a delayed report to the police, which suggests that a decision to report may in some cases be partly related to the need to obtain a crime number for insurance purposes.

- Other reasons for delayed reporting uncovered in the victims' statements examined, included the reluctance of some victims to get involved (in the case of children, often on the advice of their parents), because victims were too busy, because they didn't see what the police could do, or because they have told the police they did not regard what had happened to them as that serious a matter. These same factors have also been shown in research elsewhere to contribute to non-reporting of experiences of crime, including robbery (Simmons et al, 2002).

4   The robbery event

Although a defining feature of personal robbery is that force or the threat of force is used, the offence varies in its nature and seriousness. Thus a handbag snatch that causes injury to an elderly victim will, for recording purposes, be categorised alongside an incident of school-related bullying where no injury is caused. In short, the official record of robbery against the person does not offer much by way of insight into how these events unfold, nor any understanding of the patterns and differences that will exist within this generic crime classification.

This chapter helps unpick differences in robbery incidents by describing the more detailed analysis of the crime reports and witness statements that comprised the BCU sample. Of interest is what actually happened when victims were targeted by their attackers, where they were targeted and at what time, how their property was removed, the use of weapons and injuries sustained by victims. The analysis offers one way of reconstructing the robbery event and developing a more informed insight into the nature of personal robbery in England and Wales.

Personal robbery by time of day

Typically, robbery is more likely to occur at night.[18] Over half (51%) of all robberies occurred between the hours of 6 p.m. and 2 a.m. (Figure 4.1). A quarter of all robberies occurred in the afternoon, between the hours of 2 p.m. and 6 p.m. Half (49%) of all personal robberies occurred at the weekend.[19] Differences between the BCUs sampled may be explained by the geography of different areas, for instance the presence or absence of a night-time economy. Almost three-quarters of personal robberies in Westminster occurred at night, for example (Figure 4.2). The second sweep of Lambeth also showed a substantial proportion of robberies occurring at night. This may be explained by the variety of evening entertainment venues in these areas.

---

18.   Night-time is defined as the period from 6 p.m. to 6 a.m.
19.   The weekend is defined as the period between 6 p.m. on a Friday and 6 a.m. on a Monday. This is the definition used in the British Crime Survey.

Figure 4.1:   Personal robbery by time of day

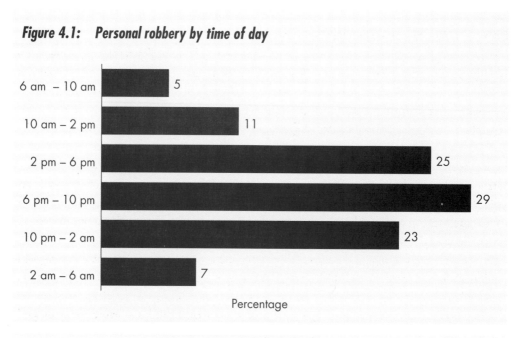

Percentage

Figure 4.2:   Night and day-time robbery by BCU/BTP area.

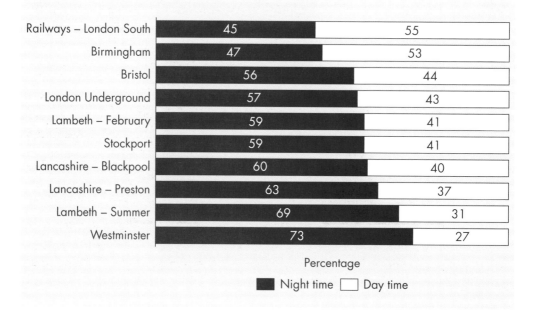

Percentage

■ Night time □ Day time

Targeting of victims by employment status

Particular types of victim, such as employed persons or children of school age, were more likely to be targeted at certain times. The employment status of a victim as one key measure of 'difference' sets the parameters of a victim's typical daily activity, determining which places they are likely to be and what they will be doing at any particular time. This, in turn, will determine the likelihood and the circumstances in which such victims are targeted.

Figure 4.3 shows that school-age and retired victims were most likely to be victims of personal robbery during the day-time, in marked contrast to the overall picture of victims typically being targeted at night (59% of victims were targeted at night). Over half (54%) of school-age victims were robbed during the afternoon period between 2.00 pm and 6.00 pm (Table 4.1). This was also the peak time in which retired people were targeted (33%). Victims who were either employed, students or unemployed were more commonly targeted at night. This was particularly the case among employed victims, of whom three quarters (74%) where targeted at night, one-third between the hours of 10 p.m. and 2 a.m. Two out of every five robberies occurred at the weekend, though robberies involving employed victims or students were more likely to do so (Figure 4.3).

Figure 4.3:   Time of robbery by employment status

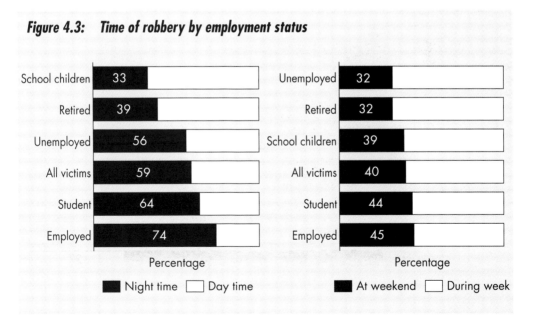

Table 4.1: Victims by employment status and time of robbery

Percentages

Time of day	Employed	Unemployed	Retired	Student	School children	All victims
0600 hrs- 1000 hrs	5	6	8	1	4	5
1000 hrs- 1400 hrs	7	22	20	8	9	10
1400 hrs- 1800 hrs	15	16	33	28	54	26
1800 hrs- 2200 hrs	28	21	26	28	27	26
2200 hrs- 0200 hrs	33	27	10	26	6	24
0200 hrs-0600 hrs	13	8	3	10	0	8
All victims %	100	100	100	100	100	100
Total N All offences	*426*	*158*	*89*	*147*	*503*	*1323*

Notes:
1. Missing = 394. Some forces do not record data on employment status, and some forces that do, do not always record it reliably.
2. In cases involving more than one victim, only the first victim is counted.
3. Night time is defined as 1800 hrs- 0600 hrs; Day time as 0600 hrs to 1800 hrs.
4. Weekend is defined as Friday 6pm to Monday 6 am (as per BCS); Weekday defined as Monday 6am to Friday 6pm

Employed persons are less likely to be victims of personal robbery during working hours because work typically places them in controlled, private and familiar spaces. Evening time brings greater risks, as victims make use of less familiar, less controlled, more public spaces to either make their way home or, perhaps, to socialise with friends. This latter point is borne out by the fact that 13 per cent of employed victims were drunk at the time of the robbery, though many more had been drinking during the evening time. The presence of 'motivated' offenders, a suitably 'vulnerable' victim, and the absence of a suitable deterrent converge in time and place and create the opportunity for robbery (see Felson and Clarke, 1998).

Similarly, the risk period for victims of school age is late afternoon when, in many cases, they will be making their way home from school or similarly socialising with friends. Parental and school guardianship constrains the activities of school-age victims and makes the opportunities for victimisation more tightly bounded to particular times of the day. The activities of more elderly persons will undoubtedly be constrained by their inclination not to venture out at night. Among these groups, victims were often targeted while making short journeys to local shops and when collecting their pension or other benefits. The routines of the unemployed and students may be less predictable, and this may be reflected to some degree in Table 4.1. A substantial proportion of both groups were victims between the hours of 6.00 pm and 2.00 am, but one in five unemployed persons were victims between the hours of 10.00 am and 2.00 pm.

The location of personal robberies

Table 4.2 gives details of the location of personal robberies as they were categorised for the purposes of this study.[20] A large number of personal robberies occurred in open public spaces, primarily a street, but also footpaths, alleyways, subways and parks. This is not particularly surprising since personal robbery is synonymous with the 'street'. Almost 40 per cent of personal robberies occurred either in or around locations other than a street, such as commercial premises or while the victim was using some form of transport. Commercial premises, which included retail premises and leisure complexes, pubs, night-clubs, and fast-food outlets, provided the back drop for 16 per cent of personal robberies. There were some marked differences between BCUs and, in some areas, offences were concentrated in a handful of specific locations. In Birmingham City Centre, 40 per cent of personal robberies occurred in or around one shopping mall and nearby amusement arcade. Stockport also had over one in five robberies occurring in a nearby shopping arcade, which included a bowling alley, leisure complex and amusement arcade. In Westminster, public houses, night-clubs and fast-food restaurants were common locations for these robberies.

Table 4.2 excludes those robberies that occurred in the two British Transport Police force areas. Nonetheless, in the other seven BCUs, a robbery occurring while the victim was using public transport was the third most frequent location type for personal robbery, accounting for 8 per cent of all robberies. Stockport had the highest proportion of personal robberies occurring on public transport outside the two BTP areas (14%), and many of these occurred on one particular bus route. One in ten personal robberies in Lambeth (both sweeps), and 7 per cent in Westminster occurred when the victim was using public transport, most commonly when leaving a tube station. However, this is an under-estimate as many 'street' victims in these areas had been followed some distance when leaving a tube or railway station.

---

20. A specific coding frame was used to record this information, and priority was given to particular location types such as licensed premises and public transport.

Table 4.2: Location of personal robbery

		As % of all personal robbery
Open public spaces	Street	50
	Subway/underpass	2
	Open space, park, common	4
	Alleyway, footbridge, footpath	5
In or around premises	Commercial premises *Includes public house, night-club, retail premises and off licenses, banks and building societies, and restaurant (inc. fast food).*	16
	School or college	1
	Other public buildings *Includes public toilets, hospitals and clinics*	2
	Residential *Includes home (or hostel) of victim, suspect or third party, and associated points of entry.*	6
Using transport	While using public transport	8
	While using private vehicle	4
Other location		2
	Total %	100
	Number of offences	*1,462*

Notes:
1. N= 1,462; Missing data = 465
2. Robberies occurring in the two British Transport force areas are excluded from this table.

The locations of personal robberies in the two British Transport Police areas, which included the London Underground and the South-East Railways, are detailed in Table 4.3. Over half (56%) of all personal robberies occurred in the carriage of the train or tube train. Over one in five (23%) occurred on station platforms (Table 4.3). Previous research has shown that the nature of robbery in these locations has changed over the last decade. Recorded robbery peaked around 1987 and has never returned to these levels (Webb and Laycock, 1991). This reduction is, in part, attributed to the introduction of CCTV and automatic ticketing barriers on underground stations. However, security measures are not as common on train or tube carriages, and this may encourage some offenders who often commit their robberies between train and tube stops, making their getaway when the train pulls into the next station.

Table 4.3: *Location of personal robberies in two BTP areas: London Underground and London South.*

Location	As % of all personal robbery
Tube or train carriage	56
Platform	23
Station forecourt	5
Booking hall	4
Subway or underpass	4
Stairs (not escalators)	4
Other	5
Total	100
Total number of offences	*288*

Notes
1. N = 288, Missing = 6
2. 'Other' includes waiting rooms, escalators, and public toilets

The initial approach to the victim

Suspects approached and initiated contact with their victims in different ways. In some cases physical force was used to stun, overwhelm or control the victim before their property was removed. Some victims were simply confronted by the suspect with a demand to hand over their property, while others were initially distracted or lulled into a false sense of security allowing their attackers time to assess their suitability as a victim. In other cases, the suspect made a grab for property that the victim had on display, such as a mobile phone, wallet or handbag. In this study, these four methods of engaging the victim of a robbery have been described as the 'Blitz', the 'Confrontation', the 'Con', and the 'Snatch'.[21] A small number of cases where identified whereby contact was initiated by the victim, and not the suspect. These cases were referred to as 'victim initiated' robberies. These five categories of victim targeting are summarised in Table 4.4.

---

21. The coding of a suspect's initial approach to the victim has been adapted from a study into linking serious sexual assaults (Grubin et al, 2001). This sought to categorise the crime into distinct types based on the way in which the different behaviours that comprise the attack group together. In particular, Grubin et al's analysis looked at how offenders gained control of their victim and how the attack was carried out. While Grubin et. al.'s work involved more complex analyses, documenting how offenders initially approached and 'targeted' victims along with other features of the attacker's interaction with the victim has proved useful in the development of this analysis.

Table 4.4: How victims of personal robbery are initially approached by the suspect

Type of approach	Explanation
Blitz.	Violence is used to overwhelm, stun or control the victim prior to the removal of any property or prior to any demands to hand over property. Violence is the first point of contact between the victim and the suspect. There is no prior verbal exchange between victim and offender, though threats and abuse may follow the initial assault.
Confrontation.	A demand for property or possessions is the initial point of contact between the victim and offender, e.g. "Give me your money and your mobile phone." This may be followed through with threats and, on occasion with force.
Con.	The suspect "cons" the victim into some form of interaction. This typically takes the form of some spurious conversation, e.g. "Have you got a light/the time mate?" This is the initial approach to the victim regardless of how the robbery subsequently develops.
Snatch.	Property is grabbed from the victim without prior demand, threats or physical force. This is the initial contact between the victim and the suspect. Physical force is used to snatch property from the victim, which is nearly always on display, e.g. handbag. There is no physical search of the victim by the suspect.
Victim initiated.	The victim initiates contact with the suspect and becomes the victim of a robbery, e.g. a drug deal, procuring sex etc.

Blitz and snatch robberies involve the least interaction between victim and offender, and the greatest element of surprise. The victim is typically approached from behind, the robbery is executed with speed, and the victim's recollection of their attackers is often limited. In these cases, contact is initiated when the suspect either attacks the victim or attempts to grab property visible on the victim's person. In blitz robberies, physical violence is used first to control or stun the victim, and then the victim's property is removed. In snatch robberies, the use of force is initially limited to grabbing hold of property visible to the offender and snatching it from their grasp, or pulling on the victim's property until they let go. Violence may follow, should the victim resist.[22] The following two cases provide examples of a blitz and a snatch related robbery.

---

22. Snatch' offences were recorded as robbery because the incident began as a snatch, with initial force being applied to the property, but force was subsequently used against the victim thus fulfilling the criteria of robbery. However, there exists a degree of overlap between 'snatch' robberies and theft from the person, caused by differing interpretations of Home Office counting rules both between and within police forces.

The victim was drunk and on his way home from a night-club when he was approached from behind by two males. He was pushed to the ground and punched and kicked. The victim's watch was then ripped from his wrist. The second male just stood and watched and did not take part in the robbery. The victim believed a knife was used to cut his face but he did not actually see it. The victim says he would not recognise the suspects again. [Blitz]

The victim was walking down the street and was using her mobile phone when the offender approached from behind and grabbed her phone from her right hand. The phone dropped onto the floor and the victim and the offender both made a grab for it. The offender elbowed the victim in the face and managed to grab the phone. The victim appeared traumatised by the incident. [Snatch]

Confrontation and con robberies typically involve a greater degree of interaction and face-to-face contact between the victim and offender. A higher proportion of these two types of robbery resulted in an offender being identified by the police.[23] In confrontation robberies, the suspect initiates contact with the victim by making demands for him or her to hand over property. These demands can include requests made repeatedly, and in a threatening manner, for 'loans' of cash or for the victim to tell the suspect what property they have in their possession. Confrontation robberies are more frequently accompanied with the threat of violence and the displaying of weapons to back up the suspect's demands. In con robberies, the suspect engages the victim in spurious conversation, such as asking for the time, or for a cigarette. The victim is temporarily distracted, and sometimes lulled into a false sense of security. The con allows the suspect time to assess the victim's suitability for robbery, and to keep the victim in situ until a suitable moment arises for them to be relieved of their possessions.

The victim went into Birmingham City Centre with his five friends. They were walking towards the shopping centre, going down the stairs into a subway and became aware of a group of three to four youths behind them. One of these youths barged through the group and stood in front of the victim and his friends. The victim thought that he was going to be robbed, so he walked around this male but was then stopped and surrounded by another male from the group. This male said: "Give me your money and your phone." The victim handed over £20 and then ran off from the group and from his friends. The victim met up with his friends five minutes later, and reported what had happened to a security guard. [Confrontation]

---

23.   An offender was identified in 15 per cent of confrontation and con robberies compared to 11 per cent for blitz and snatch robberies.

The victim was walking home after work when he was approached and offered drugs, which he refused. The offender then asked if he could use his phone which, before the victim could answer, he took. The offender started making calls on it and refused to give it back. The offender and the victim then passed a motorist who asked for a push but the offender carried on walking. Once at the beginning of an alleyway the offender told the victim to stop annoying him. The victim asked for his SIM card but the offender gave him another one out of his pocket. The offender then told the victim that, if he continued to "annoy" him, he would "regret it when he was layed out." The victim was fearful that a knife was going to be produced. [Con]

A confrontation was the most frequent method by which victims were targeted by suspects, accounting for over a third of all robberies (37%). The blitz approach accounted for a quarter (25%), and a slightly lower proportion (22%) of robberies were preceded by the 'con'. Snatch robberies accounted for 14 per cent, while victim initiated robberies made up just a small proportion (2%) (see Figure 4.4).

Figure 4.4: Type of initial approach by suspect to victim for personal robbery

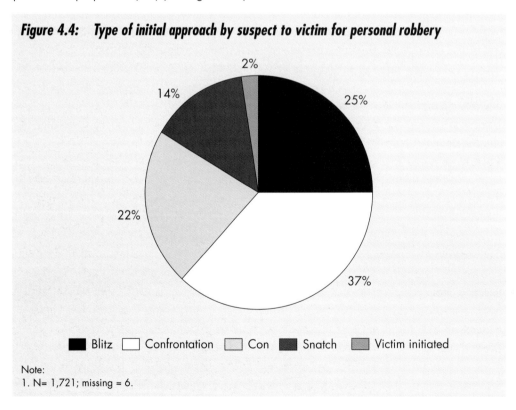

Note:
1. N= 1,721; missing = 6.

There are marked differences between male and female victims and the type of approach. Confrontation and con robberies were more common among male victims, and snatch robberies much more common among female victims. There was no real difference between male and female victims targeted in blitz robberies (Table 4.5).

Table 4.5: *Type of initial approach by gender of victim*[24]

	Column Percentages	
	Male Victims	Female Victims
	%	%
Blitz	25	25
Confrontation	41	25
Con	25	12
Snatch	6	37
Victim initiated	3	1
Total %	100	100
Total N all offences	*1290*	*431*

Notes
1. N = 1721, Missing = 6

The initial approach by age of victim

There were also marked differences in how victims of different ages were targeted. The previous chapter demonstrated how robbery victimisation generally was concentrated in the 11-15 and 16-20 age groups. These age groups accounted for two out of every five robbery victims, and have seen the greatest increases over the last ten years. Because of the concentration of victims in the 11-15 and 16-20 age groups, it could be expected that the different approach types for robbery would also be similarly concentrated in these younger age groups.

Confrontation robberies are *particularly* concentrated among younger victims in the 11-20 age group (Figure 4.5 shows that 57 per cent of confrontation robberies involved victims in this age group). Con robberies are also concentrated in the younger age groups, though not to the same degree as confrontation robberies. Snatch robberies, on the other hand, are typically directed at older victims (37% involved 21-30 year-olds, and 49% involved victims over 30 years, Figure 4.5).[25] In blitz robberies, the differences are not as marked as that

---

24. The coding of approach was based on the account provided by the police in the crime report, and the witness in their statement to the police. These categorisations were independently checked using the same information. Cases with coding discrepancies were re-assessed and the appropriate categorisation agreed among a group of 3 researchers that included the independent assessor.
25. 17 per cent of snatch robberies were against victims over 60 years of age.

seen in confrontation, snatch or con robberies, though a higher proportion of victims were aged over 31 years. In short, victims of confrontation and con robberies are by comparison typically younger, victims of blitz and snatch robberies, typically older. This point is further illustrated by looking at the proportion of all personal robbery by the age of victim and approach type. Figure 4.6 reveals that over one in five personal robberies in this sample involved victims aged between 11 and 20 years in a confrontation. This is by far the most prevalent of all types of robbery.

Figure 4.5:   Age of victim by type of approach.

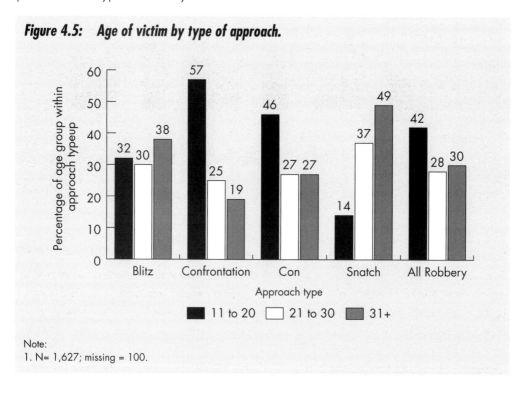

Note:
1. N= 1,627; missing = 100.

Figure 4.6: **Proportion of personal robbery by approach type and age of victim**

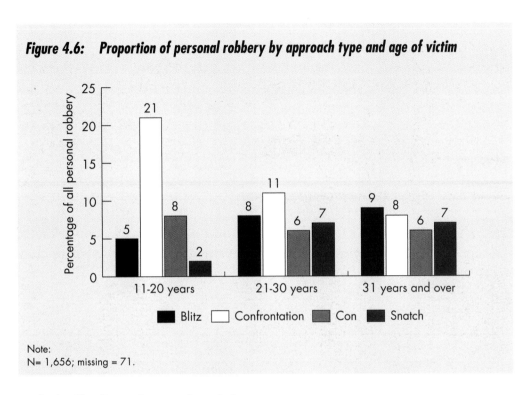

Note:
N= 1,656; missing = 71.

Multiple offending and approach to victim

Robbery committed by two or more persons occurred in six out of ten robberies recorded in this sample. Victims targeted for snatch robberies, however, provided an important exception to this observation. While multiple offending predominated for blitz, confrontation and con robberies, snatch robberies were more likely to be committed by an offender acting alone (Figure 4.7).

Chapter 3 described how victims in the 11-15 and 16-20 age groups were more likely than victims aged over 21 to be targeted by two or more offenders. Male victims were also more likely than female victims to be targeted in this way. This explains why snatch robberies were the only approach type where multiple offending did not predominate, since this is also the only robbery type where female victims outnumbered male victims.

Figure 4.7:   Multiple offending by approach type

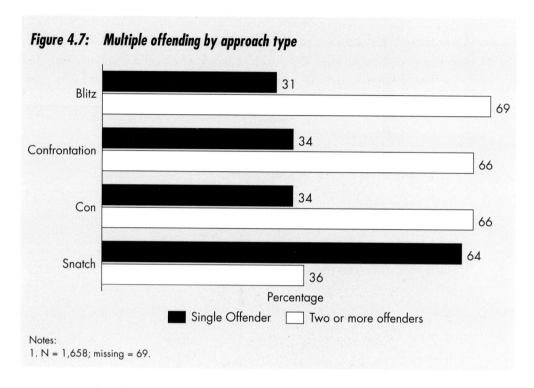

Notes:
1. N = 1,658; missing = 69.

Most personal robberies involved a single victim (90%). There were some cases where victims were also part of a group, but not all of that group were actually victims of robbery. Although the exact number of victims *and witnesses* at each robbery event was not recorded, it is clear that in most of these cases, the number of suspects was typically greater. In sum, outside snatch robberies, numerical superiority over the victim ensures that, more often than not, the robbery is a done deal.

How property is removed from the victim

Property was removed from victims in a number of ways (Figure 4.8). Some victims were made to hand over their property or turn out their pockets (28%), while others were searched or patted down by the suspect in search of valuable items (28%). However, property was most commonly grabbed from the victim's possession. This was the case in 46 per cent of personal robberies (Figure 4.8). This would suggest that in many cases, suspects took items that were easily identifiable on the victim's person and thus readily available. The various ways by which property was removed from the victim did not form mutually exclusive categories, and a victim could be both searched and forced to hand over property, for example. Most victims, however, would have their property removed in only one of these three ways.

Personal robbery was more physically intrusive for male victims than for female victims. Male victims were more likely than female victims to be physically searched by their attackers, and forced to hand over their property or turn out their pockets (Figure 4.8). Over seven out of ten robberies of female victims involved the property being snatched or grabbed from around their person. This suggests that offenders target many female victims in particular because of the visibility of the property and the ease with which it can be removed.

Figure 4.8: *How property is removed from victim*

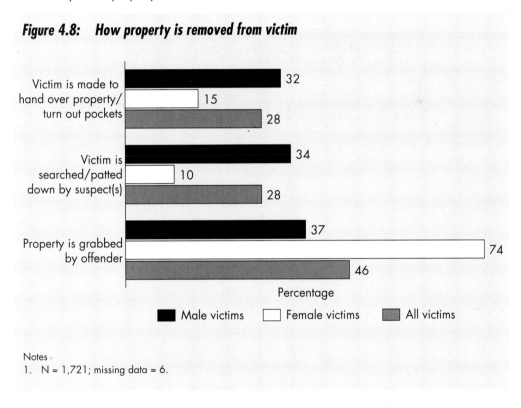

Notes
1. N = 1,721; missing data = 6.

Figure 4.9: *Use of weapons, injury, resistance by victims, and victims forcibly moved by suspect, by approach type*

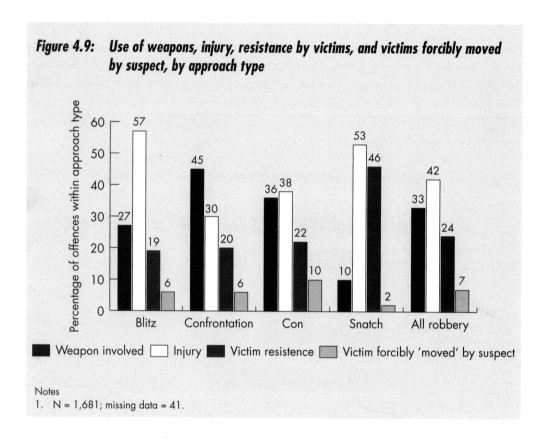

Notes
1. N = 1,681; missing data = 41.

The use of weapons

The use of a weapon does not mean that the victim was physically assaulted with that weapon. The actual use of a weapon would often be limited to its conspicuous display by the suspect, this being sufficient to instil fear of attack and ensure the victim's compliance. Only rarely would the weapon be pointed at or held to the victim's person (e.g. their throat or stomach), and rarer still were occasions where the suspect physically attacked the victim with a weapon.

Weapons were present in a third of all robberies (33%), particularly in cases where the offender's approach to the victim was one of confrontation (Figure 4.9). Knives were the most common weapon type, being used in one in every five personal robberies (21%) (Figure 4.10). Blunt instruments, which included such items as hammers, coshes, and baseball bats were used in 3 per cent of personal robberies. The use of guns in personal robbery was rare. Guns were displayed in 3 per cent of personal robberies. Other weapon types included broken bottles, screwdrivers and, in some rare cases, syringes. Together, other weapons accounted for 4 per cent of personal robberies (Figure 4.10). A small number of personal robberies (4%) involved the offender telling the victim that they had a weapon but no weapon was actually seen by the victim. Snatch robberies rarely involved the use of a weapon as would be expected given that property is grabbed from the offender without any threat or prior demand to hand it over (Figure 4.9). Men were more likely to be threatened with a weapon than women, a difference in part due to women's greater involvement as victims of snatch robberies (Figure 4.11).

Figure 4.10: Personal robbery involving use of weapon: type of weapon used

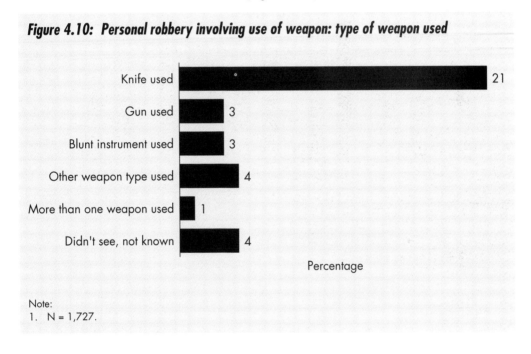

Note:
1. N = 1,727.

Physical injury to the victim

Two out of every five (43%) personal robberies resulted in injury of some sort to the victim (Figure 4.9). This was particularly the case in blitz and snatch robberies, and least likely in confrontation. This difference is most probably explained by the more frequent use of weapons in confrontation robbery, as robberies involving the use of weapons were less likely to result in physical injury to the victim. Blitz robberies are by their nature always violent and therefore more likely to result in injury to the victim. Both blitz and snatch robberies involved a greater proportion of female victims who, as will be seen, were more likely to offer resistance to their attacker. This, together with the fact that these instances were nearly always violent, perhaps explains why female victims were more likely to sustain injury of some sort (Figure 4.11).

Resistance by the victim

Victims are not always passive or compliant. One in four robberies involved resistance by the victim in the form of a physical struggle (Figure 4.9). This was particularly the case in snatch robberies, where approaching half (46%) of victims had struggled with their attackers. Female victims were more likely to resist their attacker and, probably as a consequence, more likely to sustain some physical injury (Figure 4.11). This in part explains the higher level of injuries sustained by victims of snatch robberies, since the majority of victims are female.

Figure 4.11: Weapons, injury, resistance and victims forcibly moved: differences between male and female victims

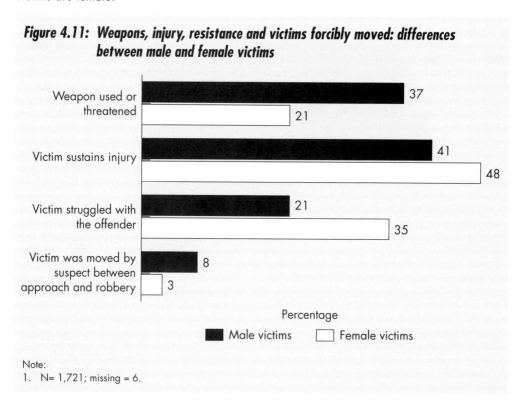

Note:
1. N= 1,721; missing = 6.

Victims who are forcibly moved by suspects

Robbery occurs quickly and the location where victims are initially approached is usually the location where the robbery takes place. In some rare cases, however, the approach and offence locations differ because victims are moved or 'escorted' to another location by their attackers (see Figure 4.9). This occurs in one in ten con robberies (10%), reflecting the fact that victims are often engaged in spurious conversation in an attempt to distract them, with some 'persuaded' to walk with the suspect to cash points or locations out of site of potential witnesses. Cash point or ATM robberies accounted for 2 per cent of personal robberies, and 5 per cent in Westminster. A small number of other cases involved victims being attacked and forced or dragged into doorways or alleyways. Such cases are few in number and the purpose of such actions may relate to the desire to avoid potential witnesses and establish control over the victim. Male victims were more likely to be 'moved' during the robbery (Figure 4.11).

What gets stolen in personal robberies?

The main motive for robbery is undoubtedly its potential for financial advantage for the suspect. The success of a robbery will largely be determined by the value and usefulness of the trawl. However, when robbery is committed by groups of offenders (and particularly among the young), it may also involve rewards of a different kind, enhancing the suspect's reputation and status among those who may know him, or her (Miller, 1998). The most frequent items of property taken during a robbery are listed in Table 4.6.

Table 4.6:   Property stolen during personal robbery

	Items recorded	As % of all property taken
Cash	986	25
Mobile Phone	694	18
Debit, credit, cash cards*[2]	337	9
Purse, Wallet	327	8
Personal accessories	312	8
Handbag, rucksack, briefcase	241	6
Personal documentation*[2]	226	6
Jewellery and watches	224	6
Other	610	15
All property	3957	100

Notes:
1. N = 3957, missing = 342
2. The analysis did not count every credit, debit or cash card, nor every item of personal documentation taken, as such items were typically removed all at once, (e.g. from the victims wallet or handbag).

Perhaps not surprisingly, cash is most likely to be stolen from the victim during personal robberies, accounting for a quarter of all property taken. Mobile phones were the second most frequent item of property taken (18% of all property taken). There are differences between male and female victims. When male victims were targeted, cash and mobile phones and, to a lesser extent, jewellery and watches were more likely to be taken. Among female victims, by contrast, handbags, personal accessories, cash, debit and credit cards, were more likely to be taken, as were items categorised under 'purse and wallets' and items of personal documentation (Figure 4.12).

These differences between men and women may, in part, be explained by the manner in which they are both targeted. Female victims are more likely to be targeted for snatch robberies and typically had their property grabbed from around their person, and handbags which would most likely contain purses, accessories and personal documentation (such as a driving licence) were obvious targets. Men were more commonly subject to physically intrusive robberies (which included being searched or being told to hand over property of value), and those suspects targeting male victims most probably chose what to take and what to leave behind when the victim was in front of them.

Figure 4.12: Property stolen by sex of victim

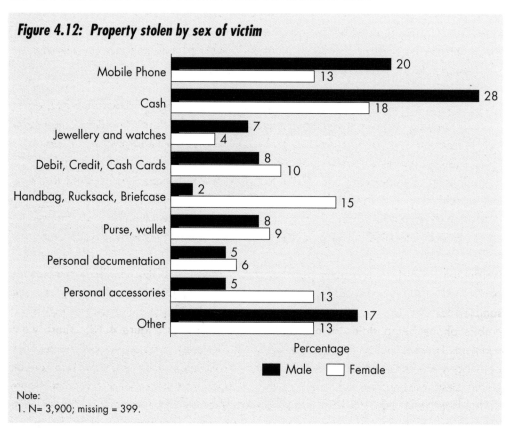

Note:
1. N= 3,900; missing = 399.

Mobile phones and personal robbery

Mobile phones have become a staple of modern day living and it was perhaps inevitable that they would become an attractive target for theft and personal robbery. A separate report has already been published (Harrington and Mayhew, 2002), which examined the problem of mobile phone theft and robbery, using a combination of police force data and some of the local level BCU data gathered from this research.[26] As the authors point out, unravelling the contribution of mobile phones to robbery is a complicated task. In relation to robbery, Harrington and Mayhew made the following observations:

- There was an increase in the proportion of robberies involving phones – from around 8 per cent in 1998/99 (an estimated 5,500 robberies) to about 28 per cent in 2000/01 (an estimated 26,300 robberies).

- The rise in phone robberies over the last two years 1998/99 to 2000/01 was generally greater than for other offences involving phones, and much greater than other offences of robbery that did not involve the theft of a phone.

- The upward trend in robbery since 1990 can be redrawn to show a levelling off in the past two years, when robberies involving the theft of a mobile phone are removed. A more stringent test of the overall robbery trend involves excluding those robberies where a mobile is the only item stolen, since this may indicate that victims are being specifically targeted for their phones, as opposed to the theft being just part of the opportunistic trawl. The redrawn trend in robbery, excluding mobile only robbery, estimates an increase of 8 per cent between 1999/00 to 2000/01 and not the 13 per cent reported in the official statistics.

Harrington and Mayhew's study provided clear evidence of the contribution of mobile phone theft to the current increases in recorded robbery in England and Wales. In the BCUs sampled for this research, over two in every five (43%) personal robberies involved a mobile phone being stolen or demanded from the victim (Figure 4.13). There were variations between BCUs. For instance, personal robberies involving mobile phones were particularly concentrated in the two BTP areas of the London Underground and London South railways compared to a much smaller proportion in Blackpool and Preston (Figure 4.13). Harrington and Mayhew observed that robberies involving mobile phones were likely to be higher in city centre areas than elsewhere. Transportation may also be an important influence on the level of mobile phone robbery in different areas. In the

---

26. Harrington and Mayhew's analysis of mobile phone robbery used BCU data from four of the sites surveyed for this research: Stockport, Bristol and Birmingham City Centres and Westminster. The data presented here in relation to mobile phones both complement and develop this analysis.

Metropolitan Police Service area, personal robberies (and theft from person snatches) have been shown to be related to transportation routes and, in particular, the location of London Underground and railway stations. Even outside the London area, with the exclusion of the two BTP areas, victims of phone robbery were significantly more likely to have been using public transport at the time of the offence.

Figure 4.13: Percentage of personal robbery involving mobile phones by BCU

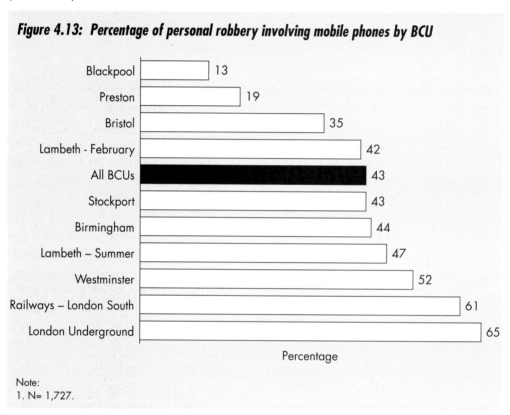

Note:
1. N= 1,727.

Personal robbery involving mobile phones divided almost evenly between robberies where a mobile phone was the only item stolen (39%) and those where a phone was stolen with other items of property (41%). In some cases, a mobile phone was demanded during the robbery, but the victim did not have one (20%). These distinctions become important when considering whether victims are targeted specifically for their phones or whether the taking of a phone was part of the general 'pickings' of people's current possessions (see Harrington and Mayhew, 2002). Robbery where a phone is the only item taken could provide one estimate of the degree to which victims were targeted specifically for their phone. Similarly, where the phone is one of a number of items taken this may provide an estimate of those robberies where the theft of the phone was just part of the acquisitive trawl. In this analysis, information was also collected on whether a victim was using a mobile phone or had a mobile phone on display (for instance in their hand), when the phone was taken from them. This offers a more rigorous definition of 'mobile phone targeting' in personal robbery, since robberies where a phone is the only item stolen may simply be a reflection of the absence of other items in the victim's possession thought to be worth stealing. Over a quarter of mobile phone robberies (27%), representing 12 per cent of all robberies, occurred while the victim was using their mobile phone, or had it on display.

Two findings lend some support to this theory. First, victims who had mobile phones taken along with other property were more likely to have been physically searched, supporting the theory that in these cases, the theft of a mobile phone was just part of the acquisitive trawl. Second, victims of mobile phone only and mobile 'in use' robberies were more likely to have their property grabbed from their person, particularly so when the phone was being used or on display (Figure 4.14).

Figure 4.14: How phones are stolen in mobile phone robbery

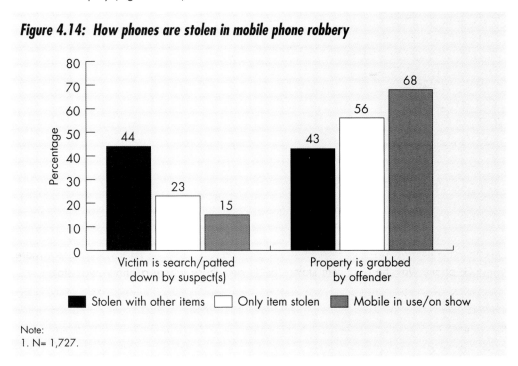

Note:
1. N= 1,727.

Younger victims in the 11-15 and 16-20 age groups were more likely than any other age group to have a mobile phone stolen. When added together, these two age groups accounted for over half (51%) of all mobile phone related robberies. Those victims aged 20 years and under were more likely to be the victim of *phone only* robberies and to have had a phone demanded from them during the course of a robbery. Those victims over the age of 21 years were more likely to have their phones stolen with other items (Figure 4.15).

Figure 4.15: Mobile phone robbery by age of victim

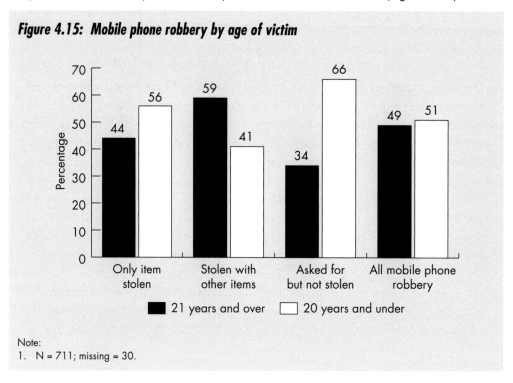

Note:
1. N = 711; missing = 30.

These differences may be explained by the fact that mobile phone ownership is generally higher among younger age groups who desire the latest mobile phones as fashion accessories as much as any practical need for their use. Mobile phones have obvious attractions for young people, not least the ability to communicate with peers on their own terms, free from parental supervision and interference. One indicator of this 'fashionable' trend is the degree to which users of mobile phones change or switch handsets in order to keep pace with new and popular designs. A survey by Oftel published in May 2001 showed that handset switching was most common amongst younger age groups, and that the reasons for changing handsets was the desire for the latest models with smaller, more sophisticated handsets (Oftel, 2001). It may well be that the possession of mobile phones among younger age groups, coupled with the desire of similarly aged offenders for the latest and most fashionable handsets will have contributed to the targeting of these age groups for personal robbery.

What else can be said about the role of mobile phones in personal robbery? Although an analysis of the motivations of those who commit personal robbery cannot be done on police records alone, there were many cases where the underlying reasons were clear enough. The following extracts compiled from crime reports and witness statements add support to the theory that the growth in mobile phone robbery is as much to do with their desirability as fashionable items, as any other possible motivation.

> The three suspects circled the victim and his friend. One of the victims was searched by one of the suspects, who removed his mobile phone from his pocket. This suspect looked at the phone and then threw it to the floor saying: "It's rubbish!" The other victim was held down by the two other suspects and punched in the face during the robbery, though no property was removed from him.

> The victim was waiting at the bus stop for his girlfriend and was sending her a text message on his mobile phone. Four males were passing by at the time. The victim overheard one of these males saying: "Check that phone." One of the other males then asked the victim for the time. The victim responded and shortly after this another six males joined the first four and surrounded the victim. Another male from this group asked to look at the phone. The victim handed the phone over to this male, who passed it to another in the group. This male removed the SIM card from the phone and placed it back in the victim's pocket. The group then left the victim, taking the handset with them.

> The victim and his friend were approached by a group of six males. One of these males demanded that the victim hand over his money and his mobile phone. The victim replied: "How do you know I've got a mobile phone?" "Everyone's got a mobile phone" replied the suspect.

> One of the male suspects patted down the victim's pockets on his jacket and removed a mobile phone from the victim's top pocket. This suspect then tried to use the phone but it had no credit, so he gave it back to the victim.

5   Discussion

Against a background of overall reductions in recorded crime in recent years in England and Wales, annual increases in robberies stand out as a disturbing counter trend. Although robberies against the person, and street crime generally, constitute a very small proportion of overall crime there is some evidence to suggest that anxiety over these crimes contributes to general anxieties over crime and policing in Britain today (Simmons *et al*, 2002). Behind the headline statistics, our knowledge of the nature of robbery, and personal robbery in particular, has been limited. This study has aimed to address this gap, through a detailed examination of several thousand police case files.

The analysis presented here has been based on a number of police force Basic Command Units from across England with different levels of recorded robbery. In some of these areas, robbery may not actually be regarded locally as a 'problem' when compared to other types of crime. The primary purpose of sampling these different BCUs was to gain some initial impressions of the common and sometimes changing features of personal robbery as well as its complexity and diversity in different areas. This chapter addresses the possible implications of these findings for the way in which police and other agencies tailor their responses to the robbery problem.

The nature of personal robbery: common and divergent themes

The analysis of nearly two thousand personal robberies reported by victims to the police revealed a number of distinctive features worth highlighting:

- Robbery is geographically concentrated within particular police force areas, and more so than other offence types. Robbery is likely to be further concentrated within BCUs, in particular hotspots such as city centre areas and transport nodes.

- A high proportion of personal robberies involved young persons as victims and offenders, and there is evidence to suggest that this has increased markedly in recent years, particularly since 1998.

- Both victims and offenders are predominately male. Group offending is the norm, with most incidents of personal robbery committed by more offenders than there were victims; numerical superiority over the victim ensures that the robbery is a done deal.

- Most personal robberies occurred in the evening or at night, at weekends and almost always in public places.

- Property was most commonly grabbed from the person suggesting that in many cases suspects took items that were easily identifiable on the victim's person and thus readily available.

- Cash is the most common form of property taken in personal robbery, but mobile phones also feature prominently and have contributed significantly to the overall increase in robbery in recent years. A previous Home Office study showed that robberies involving the theft of a mobile phone increased from 8 per cent in 1998/99 to about 28 per cent in 2000/01.

- Weapons were present in one in three personal robberies, and injuries sustained by victims in two in every five cases.

However, while common themes in personal robbery across and within our sample forces can be identified, other findings and relationships underscore its complex and occasionally diverse nature. For instance:

- The offence of personal robbery varied in its nature and seriousness. Confrontation robberies were much more common among younger age groups. Together with con robberies, they were more physically intrusive and more likely to have involved victims being 'patted down' and searched by groups of similar aged male attackers. These robberies lasted longer than blitz or snatch robbery where surprise and overwhelming force were the means by which property was extracted from the victim. Snatch robberies were more likely to involve older female victims and a single male attacker.

- Victims of snatch and blitz robberies were more likely to sustain injury. This was in part because blitz robberies were always violent, while snatch robberies typically involved female victims who more often resisted their attacker's attempts to grab property from them. This is not to say that the experience of male victims was any less alarming; they were more likely to be confronted with a weapon.

- Aside from age and gender, other victim characteristics influenced to some degree the nature of the offence encountered. School age and retired victims, for instance, were typically victims of personal robbery during the day, and half of school aged victims were victims during the afternoon period between 2 p.m. and 6 p.m. This is in marked contrast to employed victims who were much more likely to be victims of personal robbery at night.

- Even within this selective assessment of a small number of BCUs, the nature of personal robbery differs between different areas. Stockport had one of the largest concentrations of young victims aged 11-15 years, and the highest proportion of confrontation robberies. Lambeth had the highest proportion of female victims and snatch robberies. In some BCUs robbery was more heavily concentrated in particular locations such as shopping malls and leisure complexes.

While it is perhaps inevitable that we refer in shorthand to the 'robbery problem', this study has clearly identified what is more accurately described as a range of problems within different settings. Perhaps the first and most important implication of this is the requirement for high quality analyses of local problems by police forces prior to the formulation of any response. This may seem straightforward and common sense, but despite the emphasis in recent years on problem-solving approaches to crime reduction, there are still too many examples that show how police-initiated responses to problems are often dislocated from any clear understanding of them.

It is clear that robbery consists of many different scenarios involving different types of people with varying degrees of seriousness. The research offers a more sophisticated approach to categorising how robberies occur. This may be useful for operational reasons since there is reason to believe that some types of robbery are more detectable than others, and understanding how robbery occurs, when and against whom is essential in the development of crime prevention messages. It is also useful because it contradicts the everyday portrayal of 'street crime' as sudden and excessively violent, with the frail and fragile the typical victims. This is not to say that these instances never occur or that such events are trivial. But so much of what could be referred to as the new robbery problem involved youths confronting other youths, intimidating and 'fronting out' their victims, often in groups, and exploiting opportunities afforded by victim's movements, their location and the time of day.

Dealing with the robbery event: implications for the police and criminal justice system

Getting to the stage where an offender is charged with an offence of robbery can be considered something of an achievement. The investigation of robbery presents particular difficulties for the police. Robbery is a mobile crime in more ways than one. It involves quick contact between the victim and the offender. While we have not measured the time it takes to 'complete' a robbery, it is evident that compared to a domestic burglary, for instance, a robbery can be over in seconds rather than minutes. Even with high visibility policing in hot-spot areas, the opportunity for either the police or members of the public to interrupt these offences is limited. After all, some robberies may manifest themselves as little more than discreet intimidation – a police officer ten feet away may not notice what is happening. Forensic approaches are also limited, given the duration of the offence and the fact that most offences occur in public places, most typically a street, footpath or alleyway. While a quick police response is essential in apprehending a suspect, the chances of it happening in robbery are still limited.

As a quick contact crime, the visual identification of suspects has traditionally played an important part in the identifying and prosecuting of robbery offenders (Phillips and Brown, 1998). However, recent research revealed that half of identification parades were cancelled, primarily because of the failure or refusal of a suspect to attend (Pike *et al*, 2002). In one metropolitan police force, approaching half of all identification parades were for robbery. Consequently, identification parades for robbery have traditionally represented a constraining and expensive bottleneck, and a particular challenge for robbery investigations. The recent change to codes of practice allowing the use of video identification parades as an alternative to standard live parades should reduce delay and costs significantly, and be fairer to victims and witnesses (Pike *et al*, 2002).

Because the nature of personal robbery presents particular difficulties for the detection and apprehension of offenders, the police need to think creatively about other enforcement approaches. Perhaps one valuable lesson emerging from recent trends in personal robbery is the potential value in anticipating which products are likely to become hot and, critically, why they are stolen (Clarke, 1999). Analysing the 'how and why' particular items are repeatedly taken could provide useful information to designers on a product's vulnerability and the modus operandis used by offenders to overcome existing crime resistance features. Detailed analysis of hot products will also deliver shorter-term advantages in operational policing and in the delivery of effective crime prevention advice (ibid.). Mobile phones are undoubtedly the most contemporary example of a 'hot product' attractive to thieves. They are concealable, removable, available, valuable, enjoyable and disposable.[27] Each of these

---

27. These are the common attributes of a hot product. Research has shown that theft (including robbery) is concentrated upon relatively few of these 'hot' products (Clarke, 1999).

elements are important in explaining which products are stolen, and some are better addressed by changing victim behaviour, and others by design changes to the products themselves. But the degree to which they are stolen may depend critically on just one attribute – the ease of disposal (Clarke, 1999).

Tackling these disposal routes and the theft markets that support hot products is an approach currently underutilised by police forces. The market reduction approach aims to disrupt the ease by which offenders can pass on stolen goods by increasing the perceived effort and risk and thus reducing the rewards of crime (Sutton *et al*, 2001). Little is known about the market for stolen mobile phones, though it is likely that they are used either directly by the assailant or easily fenced through informal networks leaving little in the way of a trail (Burrows *et al*, 2003). However, there have been documented cases of stolen phones knowingly being bought back by retail outlets and small grocery stores, and some evidence that phones are reprogrammed using hardware available over the internet as a means of avoiding handset barring by phone companies. The recent Mobile Telephones (Reprogramming) Act 2002 will make this a criminal offence, providing a useful legislative response to this problem. In addition, studying local stolen goods markets could provide one further alternative approach in discouraging potential offenders and increasing the risk of handling and selling of these goods.

A diverse problem requiring evidence-based responses: implications for crime prevention

People's everyday movements and activities present an abundance of opportunity for theft and robbery. We can only speculate why certain victims were targeted, or why certain situations resulted in a robbery. Some personal robbery victims were clearly targeted because their attackers perceived them (or the circumstances they were in) to be vulnerable: young or elderly victims, those who were distracted, those on their own, or those victims otherwise outnumbered. Victims were also targeted because they were drunk, or simply too busy with their everyday routine to recognise what was happening around them. A not insignificant number of victims were targeted because their attackers knew that they had items worth stealing, because they had seen these items on display. On other occasions the robbery seemed more speculative, but it was a fair bet that the victim had something of value on them.

As with most crime, opportunities for personal robbery are highly specific. They are concentrated in time and space and they are dependent on people's – *victims'* – everyday movements and activity. Offenders and targets shift according to the pattern of trips to work, school and leisure settings and so forth (Felson and Clarke, 1998). As the findings suggest, the bulk of personal robbery is concentrated in the late afternoon, early evening and late at night. These three periods in which robbery is concentrated are indicative of robberies against different types of victim and different situations. Robbery in the late afternoon primarily involved victims of school age travelling from school or socialising with their friends. The victim profile changes in the evening, with victims travelling home from work being targeted. It changes again at night, as victims' use of the night-time economy placed them at risk, particularly at pub and club closing times.

The prevalence of these robbery manifestations will vary from one police force area to the next, and understanding the nature of the specific local robbery problem will assist police forces and partnerships in developing strategies to address it. There will be specific crime prevention advice to give in all these situations, focusing on helping victims and groups of potential victims to protect themselves. There is often nothing new in much of the advice to be given to victims; common sense recommendations simply need restating, albeit based on careful analysis and through the targeting of relevant groups. However, there are some findings that might further reduce the chances of groups or individuals being a victim of robbery.

Young victims as a particular target group

The large numbers of (a) school-age and (b) student victims raises particular issues for these groups. The need for effective links between police, crime and disorder partnerships and education institutions provides a crucial backdrop here. With respect to further and higher education students, several forces have already started to forge useful links with universities both in terms of delivering robbery prevention messages, as well as working closely with university security staff over police action. As regards school-age victims, one 'blanket' option might be to encourage schools and parents to dissuade children from taking mobile phones to school. This would not prevent opportunistic robberies, but a marked reduction in overall levels of mobile phone possession for high risk groups and high-risk times of day might restrict the likelihood of 'successful' encounters from the robbers' perspectives. However, there is a balance to be struck. Most parents purchase a phone for their children in order to add to their security and the natural urge to address children's risk of harm would remain, even in the absence of a mobile phone.

Alternative approaches could focus on developing protective and diversionary strategies centred on those times of the day when children are at greatest risk, namely late afternoon.[28]

---

28. There is evidence from this analysis to suggest that robberies targeting school-age children were more likely to be preceded by low level intimidation, suggestive of 'bullying' type scenarios, but this is difficult to quantify from police files. There were numerous cases were it was suggested that young victims knew at least some of their attackers but were unwilling to pursue a complaint. This may be because of concerns about the consequences of so doing, perhaps because of the fear of reprisals, or because police and subsequent court action would take longer and bring little perceived benefit to the victim.

One part of the Street Crime Initiative has involved placing police officers in schools to tackle those personal robberies that may be related to bullying, and to encourage victims to report offences. This visible presence may also provide a deterrent effect for those offenders considering targeting children outside of school, as well as providing crime prevention advice to potential victims. However, a significant problem remains with areas beyond the reach of schools popular with young people such as city centres, leisure complexes and so forth. Such locations provide a not-to-be-missed distraction for young people and potentially easy pickings for offenders.

The need to target young offenders (and potential offenders)

The growth in the number of young offenders (and younger victims) presents a particular challenge. The police are increasingly responding to this trend and more younger persons are being charged with an offence of robbery than ever before. But this also requires an appropriate preventative response. Diversion schemes aimed at providing activities for young persons need to be targeted on those who, for one reason or another, are excluded or exclude themselves from participating. That such groups of marginalised youth contribute to crime levels can be in no doubt. A recent survey by Mori found significantly higher levels of involvement in crime, and phone robbery in particular, amongst those children excluded from school (Mori, 2001). Furthermore, as was noted in Chapter 3, both the young age profile and the predominance of robbery suspects from particular minority ethnic communities in some areas highlights the need for adequate dialogue and consultation with local communities prior to and during robbery reduction initiatives.

There may also be some benefit when developing crime prevention messages in thinking through the motivations of those who commit personal robbery. Police case files offer only limited insight into offender motivation. Even so, there is evidence to suggest that material gain is not always the only motivation at play when robbery occurs. Adolescent youth perhaps more than any other group place particular emphasis on 'looking good', and the knowledge that possession of certain items may bring respectability may encourage some to adopt a less conventional route to acquiring them. There is also some evidence that robberies committed by groups of young men may be motivated by a desire by the suspect to enhance reputation and status among those who may know him, or her (Miller, 1998). These competing desires may be more tangible and relevant to some young people than legal concepts of right and wrong. Some offenders, and some victims, may not realise that what has happened is criminal. Fewer still may label it as robbery.

Recognising the geography of personal robbery

The research only touched lightly on the issue of the geography of robbery. Many personal robberies are concentrated in particular city centre areas adjacent to public transport routes and nodes. This study estimated that 8 per cent of robberies (outside the two BTP areas) occurred while the victim was actually using public transport, but definitions of proximity restrict this estimate and the role of public transport is much more significant than these figures suggest. Firstly, the high proportion of younger offenders means that public transport provides the main means of getting about. Secondly, while there have been improvements in security in stations and interchanges and to a lesser extent on trains and buses, the pedestrian routes that serve these are much less systematically protected. Thirdly, the throughput of individuals away from transport nodes gives offenders plenty of scope to identify suitable targets, and as they disperse, so this increases the chances of identifying a lone vulnerable victim. Finally, for travellers leaving sub-surface stations, particularly the London Underground, the limitations of mobile phone technology encourages people to check and use their mobile phones when leaving a station.

Overall then, an important part of crime prevention advice centres around making the public aware of the times, locations and behaviours that appear to increase risk of being a victim of robbery. The importance of the relationship between robbery and public transport highlights the need not only for increasing personal awareness in these areas, but also the need for successful police/transport provider partnerships, targeted police response supported by effective analysis, and opportunities for situational crime prevention. In many of the high robbery forces, successful efforts have already been made in these areas (further research has already been undertaken focusing in broad terms on effective approaches to reducing street robbery, see Burrows *et al* (2002)).

The study has also highlighted the importance of robbery in relation to the night-time economy. Again, in this sub-category of robbery offences, most incidents take place after individuals have been out at pubs and clubs and are on their way home. The issue of dispersal away from busy town and city centres as people make their way to quieter suburban streets comes into play here. Vulnerability can also be increased through the effects of alcohol and the data reveal that some adult victims were drunk at the time of the offence, but many more had been drinking. The fact this time of day also sees considerable demands on the police for dealing with general alcohol related disorder may place considerable logistical challenges in terms of managing the police response to both types of incident.

Victim responses to robbery

A final observation relates not to crime prevention but victim responses after an offence has taken place. Making an arrest for robbery is often dependent upon a quick response by the police and this is dependent on the victim reporting the attack promptly. While most victims reported their offence within the hour, a substantial number took longer, in some cases more than eight hours. It is right to be cautious about the reasons why some people delay their reporting. Some victims will have been injured and sought treatment first, some will be frightened or in shock, and some may have waited until they got home before contacting the police. However, other reasons for delayed reporting uncovered in this research included the reluctance of victims to get involved (in the case of children, often on the advice of their parents), because victims were too busy, because they didn't see what the police could do, or because they have told the police they did not regard what had happened to them as that serious a matter. While we need to learn more about effective robbery investigations, a clear message to the public is that, if they become a victim of robbery, if they can do so, informing the police as quickly as possible is likely to enhance the chances of an effective investigative response.

Concluding comments

Since this research was undertaken, the Prime Minister announced a concerted cross-government initiative bringing together not only the police and criminal justice agencies, but also departments of government with responsibilities for a range of issues, including employment, education, sport, transport and health. The Government's aim to bring the problem of street crime under control by September 2002 and deal with offenders quickly and effectively marked a radical step-change in problem-solving crime reduction approaches.

Developing a knowledge base on the nature of the robbery problem has played a modest but important role in shaping this process. This research provides a better understanding of the nature of personal robberies which form the bulk of what the public and media commentators alike refer to in shorthand as the 'street crime problem'. This is arguably the first step in tackling a complex and hitherto poorly understood problem. Other Home Office research has attempted to look in more detail at the police and partnerships' response to these changing crime problems and what practical and operational lessons can be learnt (Burrows *et al*, 2003). Taken together, it is hoped this new knowledge will contribute to a growing evidence base that will enable the delivery of sustained reductions in the level of robbery in England and Wales.

Appendix A: Additional Tables

Table A3.1: *Percentage change in number of victims reporting an offence of personal robbery to the Metropolitan Police 1993 to 2000.*

	1993	1994	1995	1996	1997	1998	1999	2000
White	0	12	27	37	36	20	60	97
Black	0	24	63	103	105	92	170	235
Asian	0	-4	7	22	26	17	59	97
Other	0	84	205	86	49	32	51	66
All victims	*0*	*13*	*33*	*41*	*39*	*25*	*66*	*105*

Note:
1. Shows percentage change on 1993 baseline
2. White includes White and Dark European; Black is Afro-Caribbean and 'black'; Asians are those from the Indian Sub- Continent; and 'Other' includes those ethnic groups not represented, for example Arabian, Egyptian, Chinese, Japanese, and those of mixed origin.

Figure A3.1: *Reporting of personal robberies by employment status of victim*

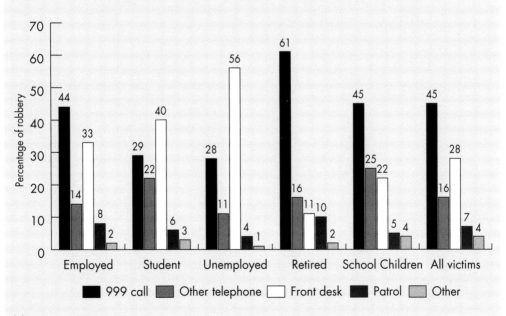

Notes:
1. Excludes 4 force areas for which accurate information on victim reporting was not available: Preston, Blackpool, London Underground and London South Railways.
2. N= 1,153; missing = 49.

Barclay, G. and Tavares, C. (2002). *International Comparisons of Criminal Justice Statistics 2000.* Home Office Statistical Bulletin 05/02. London: Home Office.

Barker, M., Geraghty, J., Webb, B. and Key, T. (1993). *The Prevention of Street Robbery.* Crime Prevention Unit Series Paper 44. London: Home Office.

Burrows, J. and others (2003). *Tackling Personal Robbery: Lessons Learnt from the Police and Community Safety Partnerships.* Forthcoming Publication. London: Home Office.

Clancy, A., Hough, M., Aust, R. and Kershaw, C. (2001). *Crime, Policing and Justice: the Experience of Ethnic Minorities, Findings from the British Crime Survey.* Home Office Research Study 223. London: Home Office.

Clarke, R.V. (1999). *Hot Products: Understanding, Anticipating, and Reducing Demand for Stolen Goods.* Police Research Series Paper 112. London: Home Office.

Coupe, T. and Griffiths, M. (1996). *Solving Residential Burglary.* Crime Detection and Prevention Series Paper 77. London: Home Office.

Felson, M. and Clarke, R.V. (1998). *Opportunity Makes the Thief.* Police Research Series Paper 98. London: Home Office.

Grubin, D., Kelly, P. and Brunsdon, C. (2001). *Linking Serious Sexual Assaults through Behaviour.* Home Office Research Study 215. London: Home Office.

Hall, S. (1978). *Policing the Crisis: Mugging, the State, Law and Order.* London: Macmillan.

Harrington, V. and Mayhew, P. (2001). *Mobile Phone Theft.* Home Office Research Study 235. London: Home Office.

Home Office (2001). *Criminal Statistics England and Wales 2000.* London: HMSO (CM 5312).

Kebbell, M. R. and Wagstaff, G. F. (1999). *Face Value? Evaluating the Accuracy of Eyewitness Information.* Police Research Series Paper 102. London: Home Office.

Kerhsaw, C., Chivite-Matthews, N., Thomas, C. and Aust, R. (2001). *The 2001 British Crime Survey, First Results, England and Wales.* Home Office Statistical Bulletin 18/01. London: Home Office.

OFTEL (2001). *Consumers' use of mobile telephony: Summary of Oftel residential survey.* Http://www.oftel.gov.uk/publications/research/2001

Maguire, M. (1996). *Street Crime.* The International Library of Criminology, Criminal Justice and Penology. Aldershot: Dartmouth.

Miller, J. (1998). "Up it up: Gender and the Accomplishment of Street Robbery." *In Criminology,* 36 (1), pp 37-66.

Mori (2001). *Youth Survey 2001.* Research Study conducted for the Youth Justice Board.

Phillips, C. and Brown, D. (1998). *Entry into the Criminal Justice System: A Survey of Police Arrests and their Outcomes.* Home Office Research Study 185. London: Home Office.

Pike, G., Brace, N. and Kynan, S. (2002). *The Visual Identification of Suspects: Procedures and Practice.* Policing and Reducing Crime Unit Briefing Note 02/02. London: Home Office.

Povey, D., and colleagues (2001). *Recorded Crime England and Wales, 12 months to March 2001.* Home Office Statistical Bulletin 12/01. London: Home Office.

Simmons, J. (2000). *Review of Crime Statistics: A Discussion Document.* London: Home Office.

Simmons, J. and colleagues (2002). *Crime in England and Wales.* Home Office Statistical Bulletin 07/02. London: Home Office.

Smith, M. J. and Clarke, R. V. (2000). Crime and Public Transport. *Crime and Justice: A Review of Research,* 27, pp. 169-233.

Stockdale, J. and Gresham, P. (1998). *Tackling Street Robbery: A Comparative Evaluation of Operation Eagle Eye.* Police Research Group: Crime Detection and Prevention Series Paper 87. London: Home Office.

Sunday Telegraph (2002). *Police fear crime explosion as school age muggers graduate to guns.* Article by John Steele published 3rd January 2002

Sutton, M., Schneider, J. and Hetherington, S.(2001). *Tackling Stolen Goods with the Market Reduction Approach*. Crime Reduction Research Series Paper 8. London: Home Office.

Waddington, P. A. J. (1986). "Mugging as a Moral Panic: A Question of Proportion." *In British Journal of Sociology*, XXXVII, pp 245-59.

Webb, B. and Laycock, G. (1991). *Reducing Crime on the London Underground*. Crime Prevention Unit Paper 30. London: Home Office.

RDS Publications

Requests for Publications

Copies of our publications and a list of those currently available may be obtained from:

> Home Office
> Research, Development and Statistics Directorate
> Communication Development Unit
> Room 275, Home Office
> 50 Queen Anne's Gate
> London SW1H 9AT
> Telephone: 020 7273 2084 (answerphone outside of office hours)
> Facsimile: 020 7222 0211
> E-mail: publications.rds@homeoffice.gsi.gov.uk

alternatively

why not visit the RDS web-site at
> Internet: http://www.homeoffice.gov.uk/rds/index.htm

where many of our publications are available to be read on screen or downloaded for printing.